CALLAGHAN: THE ROAD
TO NUMBER TEN

CALLAGHAN

The road to Number Ten

**PETER KELLNER and
CHRISTOPHER HITCHENS**

CASSELL
LONDON

CASSELL & COMPANY LIMITED
35 Red Lion Square, London WC1R 4SG
and at Sydney, Auckland, Toronto, Johannesburg,
an affiliate of
Macmillan Publishing Co., Inc.,
New York

First published 1976

ISBN 0 304 29768 2

Printed in Great Britain by
The Camelot Press Ltd, Southampton
F876

Contents

Acknowledgements

The idea for this book grew out of an extended profile of James Callaghan in the *Sunday Times*, and a study of his foreign policy record in the *New Statesman*. We believed that his career deserved more detailed attention than it is possible to give in one, or even a series, of newspaper articles. The chapters which follow do not however, constitute an exhaustive biography of the Prime Minister; our intention has been to write a *political* profile, and we only discuss his life outside politics where we feel this helps to explain his career.

We should stress that this is an unauthorised profile. Mr Callaghan found that the pressures of his office made it impossible to see us; his staff at 10 Downing Street, however, did help us with points of detail.

The generous time and encouragement of many people made this book possible: Harold Evans, editor of the *Sunday Times*, and Anthony Howard, editor of the *New Statesman*, were indulgent above and beyond the call of union house agreements in the time they allowed us, at short notice, to spend away from our desks; John Barry, an assistant editor of the *Sunday Times*, guided us patiently through the prodigious amount of research he did for the original newspaper profile; and Bruce Page, a managing editor of the *Sunday Times*, gave us characteristically sharp and invaluable advice during the early stages of our writing.

After thirty, we stopped counting the number of MPs and other people currently active in British politics and trade union affairs who have helped us. They ranged from close friends and allies of Mr Callaghan to past rivals and present opponents. It would be invidious to name only a few: in any case, the majority preferred to remain anonymous.

The librarians at the *Sunday Times*, and the staff at Labour Party headquarters, Transport House, helped greatly in digging out basic source material; and the access we were given to the archives of the Inland Revenue Staff Federation helped us to learn much about Mr Callaghan's early years as a trade union official.

We naturally consulted a substantial number of books and other published documents during our research. A selective bibliography appears at the end of the book; but we should like to thank Hamish

Acknowledgements

Hamilton and Jonathan Cape, for permission to quote from Richard Crossman's *Diaries of a Cabinet Minister*, and Collins for permission to quote from James Callaghan's *A House Divided*.

We owe a special debt to Sally Kellner who, apart from keeping one of us sane, checked the manuscript. She discovered more clichés, syntactical howlers, factual slips, and *non sequiturs* than we thought we were capable of writing. The remaining faults have occurred despite her vigilance, and despite the help and advice given by many people: the responsibility is ours alone.

PETER KELLNER
CHRISTOPHER HITCHENS

I

Caesar or Anti-Caesar?

'Upon what meat doth this our Caesar feed,
That he is grown so great?'
— WILLIAM SHAKESPEARE, *Julius Caesar*

Even when nothing much is going on, a small group of people can be found opposite Number Ten Downing Street. Some are children, having their photograph taken in front of the door, as Harold Wilson did when he was eight years old; some are tourists, who have come to see a 'sight' and find a modest Georgian town house whose exterior urgently needs cleaning; and some are Londoners, passing by, who stop for a few minutes just in case Something Big Happens, so they can tell their grandchildren, 'I was there.'

Shortly before eleven o'clock on the morning of Tuesday 16 March 1976, this knot of onlookers saw a succession of black, official limousines draw up in front of Number Ten, and disgorge their passengers, almost all of them cabinet ministers. For the onlookers, and for the ministers, it signalled the beginning of a regular Cabinet meeting.

Inside Number Ten, though, what was happening was anything but regular. As James Callaghan, the Foreign Secretary, arrived, Wilson, the Prime Minister, beckoned him into the annexe by the Cabinet room. Wilson's news was simple, direct, and stunning: 'I shall be informing colleagues at the Cabinet this morning of my resignation as soon as arrangements can be made to find my successor.'

Callaghan had been told twice in the previous six months that Wilson would resign; but he found it difficult to believe—and anyway, he had not been told the date. Wilson had celebrated his sixtieth birthday only a few days earlier, and while many men at this age contemplate little else other than retirement, it was still a sprightly age by Prime Ministerial standards. Harold

I

Macmillan did not become Prime Minister until he was sixty-two; Winston Churchill not until he was sixty-five. On the other hand, very few Prime Ministers had freely chosen the day they *left* office: most were removed either by electoral defeat (like Clement Attlee and Edward Heath) or by illness and old age (like Macmillan and Churchill). Wilson did not want to be remembered as another Prime Minister who had clung to office as long as possible.

Even so, his decision to resign had been a well-kept secret. When the Cabinet meeting was called to order a few minutes after eleven o'clock, the only ministers apart from Callaghan who knew what Wilson was about to announce were Denis Healey, the Chancellor of the Exchequer, and Edward Short, Lord President and leader of the House of Commons—and deputy leader of the Labour Party. They too had been told as they arrived for the Cabinet meeting.

Wilson began to speak: 'Before we come to Parliamentary business, I want to make a brief statement. I have just returned from the Palace where I had an audience with the Queen. I formally confirmed to her a decision of which I had apprised her early in December, that in March of this year I would intend to make way for a successor, and that I would resign as Prime Minister as soon as the parliamentary party had completed the necessary constitutional procedures for electing a new leader.'

An audience can seldom have been more captive. Wilson took the opportunity to offer advice to his successor: 'This is an office to cherish; stimulating and satisfying. You will never have a dull moment; you will never get bored ... Every Prime Minister has his own style. But he must know all that is going on. Even if he were tempted to be remiss in this, the wide-open nature of Prime Minister's questions—entirely different from that of any departmental minister—requires familiarity with, and understanding of, the problems of every department and every part of the country ... Yet you must find time enough to stand back and think about the problems of Administration, its purpose, its co-ordination and its long-term strategy ...'

Six men round the Cabinet table listened with special interest, for they were to become candidates for the post Wilson was now vacating. Tony Benn had been to Oxford, and stood for left-wing policies like worker participation in industry, and more open government. Michael Foot had been to Oxford, held strong libertarian views, and was a leading member of the left-wing Tribune Group of Labour MPs. Denis Healey had been to Oxford, was once a Communist, but had subsequently allied himself firmly with western European social democrats. Anthony Crosland had been to Oxford, and was one of the most articulate exponents of 'revisionist' social democratic thinking inside the Labour Party. Roy Jenkins had been to Oxford, and believed passionately in civil liberties and the Common Market.

James Callaghan had not been to Oxford, and nobody really knew what he believed in.

How, then, did Callaghan become Prime Minister? Or, to pose the more appropriate question given the nature of the contest which followed Wilson's announcement, how did Callaghan become leader of the Labour Party?

The best text for judging his career is probably Harold Laski's book, *A Grammar of Politics*. First published in 1925, it became a major textbook, written by one of Labour's most important intellectuals. According to Callaghan, in a BBC radio interview in 1974, it was 'one of the books that influenced me very much . . . I don't know whether it's a great book or not, but I know when I first read it, as one often does with second-rate books, a new idea suddenly comes to you. I'm not saying Harold Laski's book was second-rate—I've simply no means of judging it—but the flood of new ideas burst over me and it was that which took me into politics.'

Callaghan read *A Grammar of Politics* in the late 1930s, at a time when his work as a trade union official brought him into close contact with Laski. In reading the book, like so many students of politics, Callaghan certainly learned much about the theory of government and the way the executive, legislature and judiciary interacted—or at least, Laski's view of them all. But unlike many students, Callaghan was more interested in Laski's broad message than in his detailed analysis.

In the light of Callaghan's subsequent career, two passages in Laski's book stand out. The first discusses the instability that would occur if Britain were to become a Fascist dictatorship: 'It would be a government of naked coercion; and, thereby, it would

3

fail to meet that essential test of all governments which is the transformation, at some stage, of the processes of coercion into the processes of consent.' For Callaghan, consent—the facility for carrying people with him, and not going beyond what they will tolerate—has always been important for its own sake—though it has seldom been clear what he wants the consent *for*.

The second passage of Laski's book to shed light on Callaghan concerns the role of political parties: 'The life of the democratic State is built upon the party system . . . [The party] is the broker of ideas. From the mass of opinions, sentiments, beliefs, by which the electorate moves, it chooses out those it judges most likely to meet with general acceptance . . . When the last criticism of party has been made, the services they render to a democratic State are inestimable. They prevent popular vagaries from driving their way to the statute book. They are the most solid obstacle we have against the danger of Caesarism.'

This describes Callaghan's view of the Labour Party, and his role in it, exactly. He fought against Aneurin Bevan in the 1950s, against unilateral nuclear disarmament in 1960, and against Barbara Castle's plans for trade union reform in 1969, not because he understood the issues better than his opponents, but because he understood the Labour Party and its role in British politics better.

Callaghan eventually became party leader because of this: he was not so much the candidate most Labour MPs *did* want, as the one the fewest of them did *not* want. His leadership, like his politics, derives from consent for his pragmatism rather than from enthusiasm for any specific principles. The story of his career is also the story of the party he conquered.

1912–44
Restrained Militant

'He's not an Irishman. He'll never know why they're laughing at him; and while they're laughing he'll win the seat.'
—GEORGE BERNARD SHAW, *John Bull's Other Island*

'I was treading on eggshells. Matters of protocol in particular concerned me. One was who should say grace: I settled the issue by myself saying the simple grace that we used to repeat before meals at home when I was a boy.' (*A House Divided:* James Callaghan, p. 78.)

James Callaghan seldom talks about his origins. The incident he describes above took place in Northern Ireland in 1969, at a dinner attended by both Catholic and Protestant dignitaries. It is the only glimpse of his background in a book in which he records his attitudes and actions on Ulster while he was Home Secretary in the late 1960s.

Callaghan's reticence is understandable. His father was originally Catholic, with Irish roots: his mother was a staunch Protestant. But step by step the Irish-Catholic connection has been quietly dropped from the record. Callaghan's parents were married by the Church of England; his father, born James Garoghan, changed his name to Callaghan—a more common and more easily accepted name in England; young Callaghan was brought up as a firm Baptist.

Throughout his life Callaghan has been discreet about his Catholic ancestry; and at two crucial points in his career it proved essential to be so. The first was in 1944 when he became the Labour candidate for Cardiff South. One member of the selection committee recalls: 'I said to him: "Callaghan—with that name you must be a Catholic." He was not. He said he was a Baptist. He would probably not have been selected otherwise.'

The second occasion was when he handled Ulster as Home Secretary. Nobody, so far as we can tell, knew Callaghan's background. And when he came to say grace at the dinner he describes in his book, it was a Baptist grace. Callaghan records the satisfactory outcome: 'The distinguished clerics all solemnly intoned "Amen".'

On both occasions he was diplomatic and, in a precise sense, spoke truthfully. But any assessment of Britain's new Prime Minister must probe beyond the selective truths on which he might wish people to dwell.

Leonard James Callaghan was born on 27 March 1912 at 38 Funtington Road, in the back streets behind Portsmouth Harbour. His father, having changed his name to Callaghan, had joined the Royal Navy, where he served with some success and became a Chief Petty Officer. At his wife's request he turned down an offer to sail with Captain Robert Scott's ill-fated South Pole expedition in 1911–12, because she wanted to spend more time with him in Portsmouth. Callaghan senior went on instead to serve on the Royal Yacht, the *Victoria and Albert*. Young Len—he changed to *James* Callaghan in the early 1940s—was only four years old when his father was wounded at the Battle of Jutland, and invalided out of the service. The family moved to Brixham in Devon, where Callaghan senior became a coastguard. But in October 1921, at the age of forty-four, he died of heart failure and stomach trouble.

Now the Callaghan family was really poor. Nine-year-old Len, with his mother and sister, returned to Portsmouth. Mrs Callaghan received a small lump sum on her husband's death, but no widow's pension. The experience of poverty has undeniably left its mark on Callaghan, and fashioned some of his most deep-seated political feelings. In an interview with Terry Coleman of the *Guardian* in 1970, he said: 'I was conscious we were very poor. That led to one or two things I shall not describe to you . . . I hate injustice. I hate people not getting their rights. I will go out of my way to help any inarticulate man, who doesn't know, who can't explain, who doesn't know where to go for help, who comes into my committee room. I can't stand the smooth people who come into my committee rooms and are quite capable of helping themselves. And I never find it hard to be rude to my equals. But I'm patient with the others. I've seen it from the worm's eye view.'

The immediate struggle against poverty also had a more specific result: the family became keen Labour Party supporters. Callaghan has said since: 'My mother decided to vote Labour for a very simple reason. It was that the Minister of Pensions in the first Labour Government gave her a pension of ten shillings to bring me up. As it had been turned down by the previous Tory Government, that was a good enough reason to start voting Labour. She knew that the Labour Government was on her side.' (*Sunday Express*, 4 April 1976.) That was in 1924: Len was twelve.

In the same year, Len had his first taste of routine political work—the kind which he has always liked more than most people who go on to become national figures: he ran messages for a local Independent Labour Party candidate in the October 1924 General Election. It must have been a disappointing initiation into political life: the party's national vote rose by more than one million, but it still lost forty seats and went into opposition. The Conservatives, benefiting from a Liberal collapse, swept back to power with an overall Commons majority of 223.

At this stage, however, there were few signs that Len planned to make politics his career. For if poverty had made the family instinctive Labour supporters, it also persuaded them of the overwhelming need for security. At sixteen, instead of staying at school to take a university entrance exam, he left with School Certificate in seven subjects: 'There was no choice about it. After her experience as a widow, my mother had only one idea: to get me into an absolutely safe job that guaranteed a pension at sixty. And can you blame her?'

Whether young Callaghan would have succeeded in getting into university is debatable. Others from his school, Portsmouth North Secondary, did; and Callaghan was in the top stream of three. He did well in English and history, and showed an interest in economics: the geography master, Percy Roberts, opened a special cupboard to lend him books on the subject. His maths, however, was terrible, and overall he has confessed to being a rather lazy pupil. But in the circumstances of the family, he did not have the chance to try for university. Instead, he became a junior clerk with the Inland Revenue, living in digs in Maidstone and earning 33s 6d a week—the 'absolutely safe job' his mother had been seeking for him.

Most Labour politicians can be divided by their background into two groups: 'brains' and 'workers'. Harold Wilson and Michael Foot, with their Oxford pedigree, are 'brains': George Brown and Ernest Bevin, who learned their politics in the trade union movement, were 'workers'. Callaghan demonstrably belongs to the second category.

There is, however, a sense in which the label of 'worker' politician, which Callaghan wears with obvious enthusiasm, confuses rather than clarifies things. It is apt to imply certain experiences for anyone who, like Callaghan, grew up between the two world wars: a struggle against exploitation and unemployment; active participation in the great debates on the slump and the rise of Fascism; the forging of a clear, 'practical' socialist philosophy on the anvil of trade union activity (as opposed to the 'theoretical' socialism of the 'brains'). The Transport Workers' leader Jack Jones, though outside Parliament, represents this tradition exactly. The point about Callaghan is that the cap does not fit; he is *from* the workers, but not *of* the workers.

Callaghan's job in the Inland Revenue ensured that this should be the case. By providing him with the security which he, and his mother, so desperately sought, it protected him from the slump which was about to hit Britain. Callaghan's driving force was the powerful memory of childhood poverty rather than the adult experience of hardship through losing a job, or being paid poverty wages. In a more formal sense, becoming a tax clerk cut Callaghan off from the main stream of the Labour movement. The Association of Officers of Taxes (AOT) had been forced to disaffiliate from the Trades Union Congress following the 1927 Trade Disputes Act; neither was it affiliated to the Labour Party. Although Callaghan quickly joined the union and became active in it, the union itself was almost entirely preoccupied with parochial matters, shielded from the country's economic gales and political storms.

Callaghan rose quickly in the Inland Revenue, and in the union.

In 1931 at the age of nineteen he passed an examination to become a junior tax officer. By this time he was already a member of the union's Kent Centre Committee—getting involved, he has said, because nobody else wanted to go to Canterbury for the meetings, and the union was willing to pay his fare: 'That's one of my strengths. I became interested. I was determined to know more about trade unions than anyone else. I read. I read the Webbs' book on trade unions.' (*Guardian*, 6 June 1970.)

He evidently had no illusions about the time which needed to be spent on mundane tasks—and he prospered in the union largely because he was willing to do them. A few weeks before his twenty-first birthday he organised the Annual General Meeting of the Ashford branch of the AOT. He reported, in the March 1933 issue of the association's monthly magazine, *Taxes*, that 'although the 39 members present represented a substantial increase on the numbers present last year, the attendance still left something to be desired'.

Two months later Callaghan attended his first national union conference. He moved an amendment to one resolution, and seconded another resolution. Both related to the way the Government recruited and organised tax officials: Callaghan's line was that the union should be more militant, though not outrageously so. On one issue, where the Government was stalling, Callaghan argued that instead of acquiescing in the Government's request for patience, each member of the union 'should write personally to his local Member of Parliament'.

Callaghan's speciality at this time—as it has been during most of his career since—was the powerful expression of restrained militancy. The style showed itself in an article he wrote for the September 1933 issue of *Taxes*, entitled 'The outlook for the new entrant Tax clerk': 'The New Entrant's sole gain from the Reorganisation of the Department will be a maximum of £320 per annum . . . A boy entering the Department at 17 will be 41 when he reaches his maximum! During these years, some of the best of his life, what chance will he have of displaying any initiative, powers of leadership and judgement he may possess? . . . Write to *Taxes* about it! Turn up at Centre meetings and pester your Centre Officer with it! Get resolutions tabled and sent to the executive. For delay will be dangerous.' This article moved an anonymous tax clerk to this interesting judgement in the next issue of the magazine: 'Mr Callaghan's article . . . reveals him as an impetuous, impatient, and unreasonable man in a hurry.'

Such criticism did not worry Callaghan. He now held all three of the major local union offices: he was the Kent Centre's secretary, organiser, and delegate to the national conference. And he became a leading figure in an internal union pressure group, the special committee for New Entrants (which espoused the cause he had advocated in his September article). This was, in the words of one veteran, 'the federation's Tribune group'. The arguments which raged within the union—the pay, gradings, methods of selection, and career prospects of tax clerks—have a familiar ring to anyone who has ever become involved in the details of white collar union work. Its significance for Callaghan was that it gave him his first experience of the viciousness of political infighting. The special committee produced its own paper, called *New Outlook*. One misguided article, not by Callaghan, accused senior union officials of embezzling funds. A sharp libel action followed, entirely vindicating the accused officials, and the special committee was discredited. But even though Callaghan was one of its founders, he succeeded in persuading others in the union that he had had nothing to do with the offending article, that he disapproved of this kind of mud-slinging, and that he was altogether a more responsible type of chap.

In early 1934 Callaghan moved from Maidstone to London, and started representing the London City East E branch at union gatherings. In London he could start playing a more regularly active role in national union affairs—and he did. At that year's annual conference, the twenty-two-year-old Callaghan stood for the national executive, and was successful at his first attempt. London was entitled to six places; Callaghan came fourth with 99 votes. In 1935 he came second with 117 votes, and in 1936 again second with 123.

One of Callaghan's executive colleagues wrote in the August 1936 issue of *Taxes*: 'His enthusiasm and activity were transferred [from local union affairs] to the Executive; silent, cautious, very much subdued, a novice at first—listening to debates and arguments which he told me afterwards were beyond him. He could not put a word in; to do so would have been futile. But, saturating himself in the arguments and the history of all the issues confronting the Executive, he gradually became an effective Executive member.'

That bitter-sweet verdict rings true. But it owes something, perhaps, to the fact that its author, Stanley Raymond, had just been defeated by Callaghan in a contest to become the union's new number three official, Junior Assistant General Secretary. It was to prove an important victory for the future Prime Minister.

The union had now become the Inland Revenue Staff Federation. It was not a large union: its membership in the 1930s was 12–15,000. Throughout the 1920s there had been little recruitment of tax officers; the union's young General Secretary, Douglas Houghton—himself to become a leading Labour politician in the 1960s—was the union leader of a generally docile batch of civil servants, in a safe but static occupation. In the early 1930s the service started expanding, and a new generation of tax officers— like Callaghan—was appointed. By 1936 Houghton felt that the union should add to its staff by appointing a Junior Assistant General Secretary, to work as number three under Houghton, and the Deputy General Secretary Pat Hoey. The union's 1936 conference agreed to this decision, and Callaghan applied for the job.

Altogether there were thirty-two applications, which were narrowed down to a short-list of three: Callaghan, Stanley Raymond, and Cyril Plant. When the executive debated who to appoint, the choice came down to Callaghan or Raymond. (It was, of course, by no means the end of the road for Plant: he stayed with the union, rose through its ranks, and became General Secretary in 1960. He was one of the TUC leaders who negotiated the 1975 and 1976 incomes policies with the Wilson/Callaghan Government.) Houghton wanted Callaghan, but some executive members thought him too left-wing. Houghton secured his appointment by commending Callaghan's personal qualities. 'He was smooth, had the ability to adjust to people, and was everyone's friend', Houghton recalls. Raymond went on to become a tax inspector, then left the Inland Revenue to have a formidable career outside, culminating in the chairmanship of British Rail from 1965 to 1967.

As Assistant General Secretary (the 'Junior' was quickly dropped), Callaghan is remembered as handling with efficiency a number of administrative problems, particularly those relating to 'S class' members—ex-servicemen recruited to the Inland Revenue directly after the first World War—and the New Entrant campaign in which he had been so active as a lay member three years earlier.

But he also developed great skill at handling larger political issues. The union rarely became involved in national, much less international, politics; the Spanish Civil War, however, was something on which every part of the labour movement had to have a view. But what view? The Inland Revenue Staff Federation contained widely varying shades of opinion and ideology. Houghton, and the centre and right, were afraid that the union might be divided by taking too militant a line over Spain, and then go on to take up even more divisive British political issues. Callaghan was given the task of defusing the bomb, and he did it with complete success. Once again, his technique was to make a powerful case for restrained militancy. At the 1938 conference he proposed that the union should support aid for the Spanish Medical Aid Committee, and should commend a scheme called Voluntary Industrial Action for Spain. It was enough to satisfy the left, but not too much to frighten the right. And the official union report of his speech showed how Callaghan argued an impeccably broad-left case which no trade unionist would wish, or at any rate dare, to oppose:

'He quoted from *The Times* to show that trade unionism was not tolerated in that part of Spain which had been captured by Franco, and that the aim of Franco was to establish a totalitarian state on Fascist lines in which the workers would have no right of collective bargaining. The point at issue was that if members valued freedom of association they should assist other people in other countries who were endeavouring to attain and safeguard it.'

(Callaghan's capacity for filtering the large questions of world affairs through the fine muslin of union interests did not end with Spain. In July 1940, following Dunkirk and the fall of France, he wrote: 'Unless we prevent Germany from dominating this island as well as the European continent then the Federation, in company with all other instruments which stand for liberty of thought and opinion and economic freedom, will suffer dissolution or thraldom.')

It was in the late 1930s that Callaghan's work brought him into contact with Harold Laski, one of the seminal Labour intellectuals of the time. Callaghan frequently represented union interests at meetings of the Civil Service Arbitration Tribunal, where arguments over pay and conditions were thrashed out. At each meeting three arbitrators would be present, one drawn from a panel nominated by the unions. Laski was on the panel: in 1938 Callaghan recorded that 'In recent years, Mr Laski has sat more often than the other staff representatives.' Laski was impressed by the young man's ability and fluency (Callaghan was still only twenty-six), and encouraged him to study more widely. Laski gave Callaghan access to the library at the London School of Economics—though Callaghan admits he did not use it much: 'I was only a desultory user. I was too busy.' Even so, the two men came to respect each other. In large measure it was Laski who turned Callaghan's mind to entering politics—and later gave him the chance to fulfil his ambition.

By 1939 Callaghan had established many of his credentials for becoming a politician. His union experience, his administrative and debating skills, his tactical agility in delicate situations, were recognised and respected. He had been 'spotted' by Laski. And he now had a settled domestic life, newly married to Audrey Moulton. Audrey, unlike James Callaghan, had an unambiguously middle-class background. Callaghan says 'she added an essential element of middle-class stability to my working-class insecurity'.

But however insecure Callaghan's childhood made him feel, his livelihood was not in practice in any danger. He worked for one of the most sheltered groups of British workers, and knew it. Reviewing G. D. H. Cole's book *British Trade Unionism Today* in May 1939, Callaghan wrote: 'I sometimes think that we in the civil service who are the aristocrats of the trade union movement, who enjoy a standard of life higher than millions of our fellow workers, have a duty to them to assist them to attain the sort of conditions we enjoy.' This, like Callaghan's other writings at the time, shows a basic concern for the working class. What is lacking throughout his seven years as a union official is any more developed socialist analysis of Britain's considerable problems, or anything approaching a coherent ideology. He knew which side he was on instinctively—but only instinctively.

During the second World War his instincts grew more radical. He allied himself with that section of the Labour movement which did not give Churchill's wartime coalition unquestioning loyalty. In August 1940 he wrote in *Taxes* under the title 'Freedom in Danger': 'We do not hand ourselves over bound hand and foot to the Government. We insist . . . that the Government shall take only those powers which are essential to victory—those and no more . . . We must retain the right to criticise as well as the right to applaud, the right to condemn as well as the right to agree.'

A year later he exercised his 'right to condemn' with some force. The Government published a white paper on 'Wages Stabilisation' which urged unions not to make further wage claims. It sought, in effect, a voluntary pay freeze. Callaghan wrote: 'There are several grounds which would make the stabilisation of wages at the present moment quite intolerable . . . There is a feeling that money is still being made out of the war which disturbs so many people. If we must sacrifice some of our pre-war standards of life, as we are bound to do, let the cut hit the higher income range more obviously than it has done . . . It may be true, as the apologists say, that to cut down the incomes of the wealthy to a bare subsistence level would make little or no difference to financing the cost of the war, but they underrate the value of example. The moral effect of such a step would be tremendous.'

When Callaghan wrote that, he had acquired a degree of independence from Houghton. During the Blitz, while Houghton stayed at the union's London headquarters, part of the union's staff was evacuated to Llandudno. Callaghan was one of the evacuees. As well as his ordinary work, Callaghan handled many of the problems created by the move. He was part billeting officer, part marriage counsellor, part Butlin's redcoat. He also formed a local Fabian group, getting Laski down from London to speak to them; another speaker was the Fabian General Secretary John Parker. Like Laski, Parker was impressed, and marked Callaghan down as MP material.

In March 1943 Callaghan went to war. He had attempted to join up when the war began, and was pencilled in for the army. This angered Callaghan. His father and his maternal grandfather had been sailors, and he wanted to join the Navy. 'Three weeks before Dunkirk I wrote a letter to the Admiralty saying it was monstrous. That's one nice thing about the Navy; I got a letter from the Admiralty, from a lieutenant commander RN retired, saying yes I was right, and go and ask to join the Navy again, and show them this letter.'

For the time being, however, Callaghan stayed with the union; his job was classified as a reserved occupation, and the union was unwilling to let him go. But late in 1942 the executive decided not to seek to defer his call-up after 31 December, 'in deference to his wishes, and because it was felt that the Federation secretariat should make its own contribution to manpower'. Three months later Callaghan was called up by the Navy, sent to Lowestoft, and billeted with six other men in a room. His final message to the union, in the April 1943 issue of *Taxes*, was: 'It is no military secret to say that I am training on the East Coast and that by June I expect to be serving on a mine-sweeping trawler somewhere in the North Sea.'

Even so, Callaghan did not give up his political ambitions. He continued to correspond with Laski, and began making inquiries about being nominated for a constituency. On Laski's recommendation he was quickly short-listed for Reading, but was at sea when the selection conference was held. The nomination, and in 1945 the seat, was won by a fellow pupil of Portsmouth North Secondary School—Ian Mikardo.

Callaghan's correspondence with Laski helped, unwittingly, to get him his commission. The naval censor noticed the letters, and concluded that he must be officer material. Promoted Lieutenant, Callaghan had a quiet war in Naval Intelligence and heard few shots fired in anger. For the next two years his naval and political careers ran in tandem: a loyal sailor, he was nonetheless obsessed by politics. A cabin-mate during a brief spell in June 1944 in Iceland—where Callaghan was sent by Naval Intelligence as a liaison officer with the Icelandic Government—recalls: 'He duly arrived and joined me in my cabin. Thus commenced one of the pleasanter periods of my year in Iceland. My knowledge of politics was almost nil, and of trade unions, likewise. I was soon to learn what I had missed! Lieutenant Callaghan—"Jim" from now on—obviously knew what he was talking about, and I soon realised the objects of trade unions. Here was someone with the interests of his fellow beings at heart. In fact, after a couple of weeks I was inquiring what steps *I* should take to become a Labour Member of Parliament: I got every encouragement from Jim. We talked and discussed possible post-war problems for hours, and I well remember how my whole outlook on life was changed in those few weeks.'

After Callaghan had failed at Reading, the Fabian leader John Parker recommended him to Cardiff South. The constituency had a small Catholic population, and a larger anti-Catholic one. By stressing his Baptist faith, rather than his Catholic roots, Callaghan defeated George Thomas, now Speaker of the House of Commons, by one vote for the nomination. It was a good nomination to win: Callaghan's task was to overturn a Conservative majority of only 541.

While he was still in the Navy Callaghan had little chance to 'nurse' his seat. But he was as active as the war permitted, and in December 1944 went as the prospective candidate for Cardiff South to the forty-third annual conference of the Labour Party. On the third day he made his mark, in what must rank as the most radical speech he has ever made. He was supporting Mikardo over nationalisation, and against the party executive's downgrading of it in its report to the conference. 'I think we are entitled to an explanation from the Executive Committee as to why the issue of public ownership was not included in the Report. It may be said that as it is such a cardinal feature of Labour Party policy there is no need to say anything about it. That may be true so far as the delegates here are concerned and the Executive Committee, but there are millions of men in the Forces who do not understand that public ownership is a part of Labour Party policy. I think it is high time that we should re-state our fundamental principles in a document of this sort . . . I want this word to go out from the Party Conference to the men in the Forces that unless the Labour Party is returned to power to bring in a planned system, a planned economy, and public ownership, then they will come back to unemployment.'

Philip Noel-Baker, replying for the executive, asked Mikardo not to press his resolution to a vote. Mikardo refused, and the resolution was passed. The Labour Party was now committed to an election programme which included 'the transfer to public ownership of the land, large-scale building, heavy industry, and all forms of banking and fuel and power'.

After the debate, one Labour luminary, Herbert Morrison, went up to Mikardo and Callaghan and said: 'Do you realise you have just lost us the next General Election?'

3

1945–51
The Making of a
Practical Politician

'A little rebellion now and then is a good thing.'
—THOMAS JEFFERSON, in a letter to James Madison

With hindsight, it seems odd that so few people expected Labour to win the 1945 General Election. The language of political debate during the war had been the language of radical change. William Beveridge's famous report on national insurance spoke openly of the need for 'revolutionary measures'. Although some Conservatives sailed part of the way on the tide—like R. A. Butler, with his 1944 Education Act—it was the Labour Party which most clearly articulated the mood of change. What is more, there is clear evidence from the war years that the voters wanted radical measures. Between March 1942 and April 1945 the Conservatives lost ten seats in by-elections, usually to left-wing independent candidates. (Normal Conservative-Labour competition was suspended during the wartime coalition.) And the infant Gallup Poll consistently showed Labour with leads of between 12 and 18 per cent in surveys it conducted between July 1943 and June 1945.

Yet surely on the day the people would not be so ungrateful as to reject Winston Churchill?

Callaghan spent VE day chasing a Japanese cruiser in the Indian Ocean, which is probably where he would have stayed for a few more months if the Labour Party had not insisted on an immediate election, instead of waiting for the Japanese to surrender. As a parliamentary candidate, Callaghan was taken to Rangoon, and

18

then flown home for the last three weeks of the campaign. 'It is a curious sensation', he wrote shortly afterwards in *Taxes*, 'to be whisked 8,000 miles in a couple of days and dumped down in the middle of a British General Election. The day before I left for England I was at a Naval Air Station in the jungle where the things that mattered were how to keep cool, when did the mail arrive from home, how long before we were going to be repatriated, when were we going to have another go at the Japs, and changing into long trousers and long sleeves by 7 p.m. to avoid the malarial mosquito. Exactly a week later I was addressing a meeting of old age pensioners in the docks quarter of Cardiff.'

The party programme he fought on had been slightly watered down since the conference the previous December. Even so, the manifesto, 'Let Us Face The Future', promised a 'tremendous overhaul . . . drastic policies of replanning . . . a firm, constructive hand on our whole productive machinery . . .'

The actual experience of an election campaign, however, concentrated Callaghan's mind on bread-and-butter subjects, rather than the socialist vision which he had fleetingly proclaimed six months earlier. The issues, he subsequently wrote, were 'homes, work, enough to live on when overtaken by misfortune, demobilisation, and the merchant seaman's post-war position'. Callaghan, the radical campaigner of 1940–4, had already started reverting to Callaghan, the practical man. In South Wales, though, he was still considered sufficiently left-wing for local Communists to help actively in his campaign. Idris Cox, former South Wales organiser for the Communist Party, sums Callaghan up as 'not ever really left-wing—but not completely right-wing either'. Put another way, Callaghan showed himself then, as he has shown himself since, to hold no passionate ideological convictions; his prodigious skill has been to know what is *acceptable* to the people that count on the occasions that matter.

When the election results were declared on 26 July—there had been a three-week delay since polling day to allow the far-flung service vote to be counted—the country (or at any rate the newspapers and the Conservative Party) was stunned. Labour had won 393 seats, 180 more than the Conservatives, and 146 more than all other parties combined. In Cardiff South, Callaghan ousted the Conservative, Sir Arthur Evans, who had held the seat for nineteen of the previous twenty-one years. Callaghan's majority was 5,944. Commenting on the results the *Manchester Guardian* declared the next day: 'Britain has undergone a silent revolution. Throughout the country, in country no less than town, they swung to the Left. And when they voted Left they meant it. They had no use for the middle-of-the-road Liberals; they voted Labour and they knew what they were voting for . . . It is the kind of Progressive opportunity that comes only once in every few generations.'

The question was: how would the 393 Labour MPs—and Callaghan among them—use that opportunity?

The leader of any party winning an election has to find close to 100 MPs to fill government jobs, ranging from cabinet posts to Parliamentary Private Secretaries. The 1945 election landslide gave some new MPs an immediate opportunity to be more than mere back-benchers. Callaghan was one of the lucky ones; the new Prime Minister, Clement Attlee, appointed him PPS to John Parker, the Fabian who had encouraged his political career during the War and who was now Under-Secretary of State for Dominion Affairs.

The job of PPS is really only half a government job. It requires active support for your own ministry's policies, but allows you some independence to comment on other issues. You must not rock the boat, but you may suggest politely that it steers a different course. At first Callaghan enjoyed this role. In his maiden speech, a week after VJ day, he attacked America's handling of the Japanese surrender and argued that the Emperor Hirohito should be deposed: 'A divine monarch is the embodiment of all that is opposed to a democratic State. We must get rid of him.' The Cardiff morning newspaper, the *Western Mail*, described Callaghan's maiden speech as 'one of the finest ever delivered. He spoke in such an able, well-informed manner, and with such an unostentatious, yet confident, style that when he concluded he received a spontaneous outburst of applause and congratulations from members on all sides.'

These were heady days. Callaghan was spotted by the Chancellor of the Exchequer, Hugh Dalton, who wrote in his memoirs *High Tide and After:* 'I was most anxious to collect a good group, whose members already knew something of finance, with whom

I could usefully consult, and who would be eager for action, but sensibly co-operative.' He invited Callaghan into this group, along with other promising MPs like Hugh Gaitskell and Christopher Mayhew.

Callaghan did 'know something' of finance: his pre-war work ensured that. But he was no economist, nor even an expert on taxation. Yet he served Dalton's purposes well, for he was excellent at assailing the Conservatives in Commons debates. In November 1945, during a debate on the Finance Bill, he attacked a Conservative amendment to cut surtax. Michael Foot's verdict in the *Daily Herald* was: 'One of the most brilliant debating speeches of this Parliament. It came, significantly enough, from one of the despised new members of four months ago. James Callaghan, of Cardiff, explained in words of almost one syllable how a drop of 10 shillings a week in the income of those receiving £4,000 a year would not, in his humble submission, plunge the country into ruin.'

Yet despite the flattery and the patronage, Callaghan found he was not entirely happy. If he could not have a *real* government job, he wished to enjoy the freedom of the back benches. On 13 December, along with twenty-two other Labour MPs such as Michael Foot and Jennie Lee, he voted against the Bretton Woods agreement which established the International Monetary Fund and the World Bank. Four days later he resigned as Parker's PPS. It is fair to say that in such circumstances resignation is almost automatic. But on this occasion it was not strictly necessary; Barbara Castle, PPS to Sir Stafford Cripps, at the Board of Trade, also voted against the Government, but she did not resign. In the final analysis, Callaghan resigned out of choice rather than necessity.

Callaghan's career as a 'rebel' lasted twenty-two months. Within the Labour Party today he is vaguely remembered for being militant; the record shows him to have been only vaguely militant. One index of left-wing militancy in the Attlee Government is the number of times an MP voted against the Government. Minor rebellions were then frequent, as Labour's huge Commons majority ensured that they would not bring the Government down. During Callaghan's spell as a back-bencher there were nineteen left-wing rebellions of substance—divisions in which at least ten Labour MPs voted against the party whip. Every few weeks MPs like Sydney Silverman, Ian Mikardo and Tom Driberg would troop through the lobbies to register their displeasure at the way the Cabinet was retreating from its manifesto promises over such things as national insurance, and the running of the civil aviation corporations. Some left-wing MPs who were less inclined to rebellion nevertheless joined these revolts from time to time: Michael Foot three times during this period, Barbara Castle twice. Callaghan voted against the Government only once—and that was a lone gesture, rather than part of a serious revolt. On 14 May 1947 Callaghan protested against the Cocoa Prices Order which would, he said, 'have the effect of nearly doubling the 3d bar of chocolate that we buy'.

Callaghan's rebel-index rises somewhat when his role in smaller back-bench groups is examined. In July 1947, in a House of Commons standing committee which was going line by line through a new Companies Bill, he proposed an amendment to force disclosure of nominee shareholdings, and secured a 13–10 victory against the Government. (The amendment was reversed later: today nominee holdings remain secret.) And as chairman of the party's Defence Committee, he rightly took the credit for persuading the Government to reduce the period of conscription for national servicemen from eighteen months to twelve. (The period was subsequently raised to two years when national service was reorganised to involve fewer conscripts.)

But Callaghan's half-hearted approach to the left is, perhaps, best illustrated by his relationship with the Keep Left group. One evening in January 1947 when the Commons was sitting late, about a dozen left-wing MPs met and agreed to draw up a Socialist critique of the Government's policies. Led by Richard Crossman, Foot and Mikardo they began holding weekly lunches at La Belle Meunière in Charlotte Street, to draft a 48-page booklet called 'Keep Left'; Callaghan occasionally attended these lunches. The booklet did not, in fact, turn out to be an outrageously radical critique: indeed some passages contained a somewhat wayward arrogance. ('Our concept of democracy relies on having not merely a politically intelligent people, which mercifully we have, but also a politically informed people, which unfortunately we do not.') But for anyone with serious pretensions to being part of the Labour left, it was essential to sign. Callaghan refused. For a while, he still joined in the lunch meetings. But one day in early October 1947, he took Mikardo to one side and said: 'This is the last of these meetings I shall be attending. I've just been offered a government job.'

Nobody was surprised, though some MPs were annoyed, when Attlee appointed Callaghan as Parliamentary Secretary for Transport—a real government job this time, one rung up from Parliamentary Private Secretary. Callaghan recalls that his interview with the Prime Minister lasted only two minutes: '[Attlee] said in his quiet dry way: "Remember you're not playing for the second eleven any more; you're playing for the first eleven. And one other thing: if you are going to do business with somebody don't insult him the day beforehand. Goodbye." '

One Labour MP openly criticised the appointment. C. C. Poole, a former railway clerk and by then the member for Lichfield, complained that 'an income tax expert has been sent to the Ministry of Transport when there are 50 men on the back benches who have spent a lifetime in transport'. Some jobs, he said, had been given to 'the boys' who had kept quiet and never made things awkward for senior ministers. This was an understandable half-truth: as we have seen, Callaghan had *not* kept quiet—but it is fair to say that he seldom made things awkward. Indeed, contemporaries recall his considerable skill at making vigorously anti-Conservative Commons speeches when he knew Attlee was in the chamber. Altogether, Callaghan could not have found a more effective recipe for gaining ministerial office.

During the next four years Callaghan held two junior ministerial jobs; in 1950, after Transport, he became Parliamentary Secretary to the Admiralty. In both posts he was workmanlike and modestly effective. At Transport he ran the Government's first road safety committee, and he introduced 'cat's eyes'. In his time at the Admiralty he is best remembered for taking part in early Council of Europe meetings at Strasbourg. Although he took part technically as a party, rather than government, representative, he furthered his ministry's policies by successfully fighting off an attempt in August 1950 to set up a European army run by the Council. Hugh Dalton, leader of the Labour delegation, had already told Attlee that Callaghan worked hard: 'He [has] been working up his French and, by the end, seemed to understand a lot and spoke quite passably. He is, as you know, a cheerful companion, and a very capable and self-confident young man.' After the August 1950 meeting Dalton wrote again to Attlee: 'Callaghan was definitely recognised, by me and others, as my No. 2. He disported himself well and, I am sure, learned much.'

But competence as a junior minister provides only part of the basis for a successful career. You also need to build up your following inside the party. One of the secrets of Callaghan's rise to power is that he mastered this point early on. Even as a junior minister in the late 1940s he cultivated his party base, as well as carrying out government work.

Inside the Parliamentary Labour Party, Callaghan displayed an excellent sense of timing. In May 1948 he launched a much publicised attack on Emanuel Shinwell, then chairman of the Labour Party, and Secretary of State for War. Shinwell, always a controversial figure, was going through one of his more unpopular spells because of his handling of a bitter party squabble over Labour's relations with different groups of Italian socialists. Then, on 2 May, Shinwell compounded his plight with an over-frank and consequently unwise speech in Edinburgh. He said the party had done 'far too little detailed preparation' for its nationalisation programme: 'We found ourselves with legislation that had to be completed without the necessary blueprints ... When the mining industry was nationalised—this had been on the Labour Party programme for fifty years—we thought we knew all about it; the fact of the matter was, we did not.'

Callaghan now saw his chance. At a meeting of the Parliamentary Labour Party three days later, in the presence of Attlee and a large number of other MPs, he accused Shinwell of doing the party more harm than the dispute over the Italian socialists. The point—and effect—of Callaghan's intervention was succinctly stated in the following morning's *Daily Express*: 'Normally such conduct by a junior Minister would call for severe censure. But it now seems unlikely that any action will be taken against Mr Callaghan because it is held that he did no more than reflect the view of a large number of the party's rank and file.' For good measure, the *News of the World* indicated that Callaghan had done himself no harm when on 9 May its political correspondent wrote that 'James Callaghan ... is an obvious candidate for further advancement. His friends admire him, and his enemies respect his honesty, and I believe he has too great a sense of humour to let early success make him as big a bore as some of his colleagues.'

One possible reason why Callaghan received such a good press at this time was that he had begun discarding his earlier left-wing policies. The process of disengagement from the left, which had begun with his refusal to sign 'Keep Left', was completed between 1949 and 1951.

Three episodes illustrate the emergence of the pragmatic, centre-right Labour politician Callaghan has remained ever since. The first took place at the 1949 Labour conference, when a new General Election was known to be only months away, and the party was debating how much further the Government should go with its nationalisation programme. In 1944, of course, Callaghan had called for full-blooded socialism; but this time his tune was different: 'We are going to need to be extremely flexible in the programme that we place before the country and in our methods of carrying it out ... I do not want us to feel, when we get back into power in 1950, that our first task, pre-eminent and above all, is to nationalise cement.'

The second episode concerned Aneurin Bevan's resignation from the Government in April 1951 over the decision of Hugh Gaitskell, the Chancellor of the Exchequer, to introduce prescription charges in the National Health Service. The establishment of the NHS in 1948 was one of the Attlee Government's proudest achievements, and a monument to the work of Bevan as Minister of Health. One of its cardinal principles had been that it should be free at the time of use: prescription charges ran directly counter to this principle. For more than a week after the Budget, Bevan agonised over whether he should resign. A number of MPs wrote to him, urging him not to. Callaghan wrote twice. In his first letter (signed jointly with four other MPs), he said: 'The Party's interests will only be saved if we *all* go into a general election *together*. Any fragmentary resignations will split the party in the constituencies, and we shall be not only defeated in the election— but routed.' Callaghan's second letter, a few days later, was signed alone: 'I've talked about the business again to some of my friends. Our unanimous view is that the Cabinet's decision must be accepted—and that no significant section of the Party will oppose it. Neither do we think many of the constituency parties will oppose it.'

The third episode occurred once more at a Labour Party annual conference—a forum where Callaghan has always performed skilfully, and which he has always taken seriously. In 1951 he spoke on rearmament, one of the touchstone subjects which divided Labour's right and left in the early 1950s. As a junior minister at the Admiralty Callaghan naturally had to present government policy. But he did so with evident relish, explaining his position with a homespun yarn about a boy who loses his ball over a garden wall: 'When I was a boy, I used to run back into the kitchen and say, "Mum, will you go and ask Mrs Green if I can have my ball back?" And when she did, I got it back with a smile on Mrs Green's face, because they were talking as equals. The whole purpose of this rearmament programme is so that we can match up and speak to the USSR in terms of confidence born from a knowledge of our own strength.'

When a politician changes his ideas—as these three episodes show that Callaghan did—it is noteworthy but not necessarily blameworthy. Judged by Aldous Huxley's dictum that 'the only completely consistent people are the dead', Callaghan was very much alive. The important point is not to criticise Callaghan's change of outlook, but to explain it.

Some clues are contained in the words Callaghan used on these three occasions. Over nationalisation his argument was not that it was wrong, or that in practice it had proved a mistake; it was that the party should be 'extremely flexible' instead of becoming too committed. Over prescription charges his argument was not that they were right, or even that in the economic circumstances of the country they were justified; it was that the 'Party's interests' came first, and 'the Cabinet's decision must be accepted'. Over rearmament there was no analysis of Soviet intentions, or of the alternative, cheaper policies which could be pursued—but a simple desire to speak to the Russians as equals.

Now these are all perfectly defensible attitudes. They do, however, show that Callaghan's move to the right had very little to do with deeply held ideological convictions. They are the arguments of a practical man, firmly anchored to a keen sense of what will keep the show on the road; they are not the arguments of a man greatly concerned with theory or analysis. Above all, they are the arguments of a man who reduces political ideas to issues of tactics.

The advantages of Callaghan's position are considerable. If you do not state clear political beliefs you can avoid making too many enemies. If your appeals for party unity sound convincing enough, you can actually make friends and win support. These skills, however, work most effectively when you are *seeking* power. The trouble starts when you *achieve* power. Then, if you take tactical gamesmanship to its logical conclusion you end up with entirely random policies: your chances of coming up with the wrong answer are as great as your chances of coming up with the right one, if not greater.

But at the end of 1951 these particular chickens were thirteen years away from coming home to roost. Callaghan was about to face a more immediate test of his political skills.

4

1951–63
How to Build a
Power Base

'A man cannot be too careful in the choice of his enemies.'
—OSCAR WILDE, in *The Portrait of Dorian Gray*

The Attlee Government died a sad death. In the February 1950 General Election Labour lost about 70 seats (boundary changes make precise comparison with 1945 impossible), but just managed to stay in power with an overall majority of five. Asked what he planned to do, Attlee replied tersely, 'We carry on.' For a year and a half he managed to do so, but with growing difficulty. Some Labour MPs—survivors from the Ramsay MacDonald era—were now old or ill, and tired: the 1945–50 Parliament had passed a substantial body of reforming legislation, from nationalising the railways and the coal mines to constructing the modern welfare state, and the narrowness of the 1950 majority was deeply discouraging. In October 1951 Attlee held a further General Election; Labour lost another 20 seats, and the Conservative Party led by Winston Churchill was back in power.

As in October 1924, when the twelve-year-old Callaghan had been running messages for the local ILP candidate, the result contained a sour irony for Labour. It polled more votes than ever before—and 230,000 votes more than the Conservatives. Indeed, in 1951 Labour set up a record which no party has yet broken: a total vote just 50,000 short of 14 million. Its share of the national vote was 1 per cent higher than it had been in 1945. The reason why Labour lost, then, had little to do with any crumbling of Labour support. What happened was that, as in 1924, the Liberal vote collapsed, and went overwhelmingly to the Conservatives, who managed to secure 26 more seats than Labour, and return to government with an overall Commons majority of 17.

But however unfair the rules may seem, a defeat is a defeat, and Labour went into opposition. Labour Party politics are very different in government and opposition. In government, most of the power filters down from the top, through the patronage of the Prime Minister and the decisions of his Cabinet. The main function of MPs is to sustain the Government with their votes, however critical they may be with their speeches. (There is a sophisticated etiquette concerning rebellions; the cardinal principle is that whatever you do, you do not bring the Government down.) Outside Parliament, National Executive elections are held, and party committees meet as usual. But in the end they can only advise or, if they feel strongly, growl. That is all: they have no real power.

In opposition, the facts of Labour life are very different. Power is more dispersed. While a Cabinet is in the gift of a Labour Prime Minister, the shadow cabinet is essentially elected by Labour MPs, who vote for twelve places. Technically the vote is for a Parliamentary Committee; the full shadow Cabinet is completed with the addition of people invited by the leader. The point remains that if you want to build a secure career in opposition, you need to hold one of the *elected* places. Outside Parliament, the National Executive becomes much more important when Labour is in opposition. Its *formal* powers are no different, but its influence, especially over policy-making, is far greater. This in turn gives added importance to the people who elect the Executive—the constituency parties and the trade unions.

The difference between Labour in government and Labour in opposition is crucial to any understanding of Callaghan's career. Up to 1951 he had progressed by showing ministerial competence, and by impressing leading Labour figures such as Laski and Dalton. He had cultivated wider support within the Parliamentary Labour Party (for example over the Shinwell row), but this had not been strictly essential for his advancement. From 1951 to 1964 it was an absolute necessity to build as broad a base as possible.

Callaghan's success during those years was formidable. He was the only Labour MP to be elected to the shadow cabinet every year; he also developed a steady following in the constituency parties. It is worth setting out his record in detail:

YEAR	SHADOW CABINET		NATIONAL EXECUTIVE [NEC]	
	Place (first twelve elected)	*Vote*	*Place* (first seven elected)	*Vote* ('000s)
1951	7	111	—	—
1952	6	137	10	196
1953	4	160	10	315
1954	10	124	8	495
1955	3	148	(did not stand)	
1956	5	140	8	558
1957	5	171	7	565
1958	5	150	7	583
1959	2	149	6	606
1960	1	159	6	530
1961	7	156	7	528
1962	1	164	8	444
1963	2	175	6	562

No other Labour MP can match the *consistency*, let alone success, of this record. It meant a lot to Callaghan, for his one constant political *credo* has been the importance of a strong, united Labour Party. Instead of espousing specific policies or great causes, Callaghan loves the party, and he wants the party to love him. (His one failure to secure re-election to the NEC after 1957 occurred in 1962—and this owed more to the sudden popularity of Anthony Wedgwood Benn than to any real coolness towards Callaghan.)

Callaghan's performance was especially notable, for although he had made useful progress between 1945 and 1951, he was still some way down the party's pecking order. Only two junior ministers had lost their seats in the 1951 General Election, so there were at least forty former Cabinet and non-Cabinet ministers who could claim seniority over Callaghan. Youth, however, was on his side—he was now thirty-nine—and he could argue that any future Labour Government would have to be built round men of his generation. Callaghan decided to stand in the first shadow cabinet election a few weeks after Labour was defeated. The result was remarkable: he came seventh with 111 votes.

Everyone else to be elected had held senior ministerial office, and he secured more votes than even his mentor, Dalton, and his enemy, Shinwell.

In the 1950s and early 1960s, moreover, it was no easy trick to hold a large following in both the PLP and the constituencies. Among MPs the centre and right were always in a majority; but the constituencies were by some distance more left-wing. In the late 1950s, when Callaghan became elected to the NEC, only Harold Wilson and Anthony Greenwood could share his claim that they had the support of both MPs and constituency workers. Others built up support among one, but not both: Tom Fraser, Sir Frank Soskice, Denis Healey, for example, among MPs in shadow cabinet elections; Ian Mikardo, Barbara Castle, Richard Crossman in NEC elections.

How did Callaghan do it? We must start with an analysis of his role in the vital controversies involving Aneurin Bevan, which dominated Labour Party politics in the early 1950s.

Callaghan's support came chiefly from the centre and right of the party, with which he had aligned himself during the previous three years. Inside the shadow cabinet he lined up against Aneurin Bevan and the left. This consolidated his support among MPs— his vote reached a temporary peak in 1953 when he came fourth— but risked alienating support in the constituencies, where Bevan was much more popular.

It was a risk Callaghan was prepared to take, and he became one of the anti-Bevan hawks. At the 1952 party conference in Morecambe he openly accused the Bevanites of being less than candid with their own supporters. Bevan sympathisers had won six of the seven places on the NEC chosen by the constituencies. The day after these results were announced, Callaghan said, during a debate on defence policy, 'The sweeping Bevanite victory yesterday calls upon the Bevanites to make certain decisions and to state their position clearly in a way in which they have not done so far . . . I want to put it to them in this way. I think they are in danger of intellectual hypocrisy. Let them be aware of this. I am really addressing the six Bevanites, almost more than their supporters, but I will address them through this conference. They have got to power believing that the North Atlantic Treaty is the keystone of our defence, but many of the people who voted for them do not believe anything of the sort ... I believe that our democratic Socialism is the best way of life for all of us. That is what I want to preserve. That means armaments; it means an alliance with the United States of America. It does not mean I do not criticise America ... But it does mean that we [must be] aligned with forces who are against the insidious attempts of communism to break the democratic Socialist movement.' For the height of the cold war this was heady stuff; and if Callaghan was in danger of alienating the constituency vote, his speech went down well with the conference as a whole. Dominated by the mainly right-wing block votes of the big trade unions, the conference backed the Attlee leadership against the left.

On one issue, however, Callaghan lined up with the Bevanites: like them, he opposed German rearmament. This argument cut across simple right–left lines: for people like Callaghan the fear was that allowing rearmament would increase the risk of war; people like Herbert Morrison, on the other side, feared that *not* to allow rearmament would appear vindictive to the Germans, repeating the mistakes made following the first World War. At first, the opponents of rearmament held a majority in the shadow Cabinet and PLP. But in February 1954 a resolution supporting German rearmament was approved by the PLP by 113 votes to 104. For one of the few times in his career, Callaghan was on the losing side of a major PLP policy vote.

The rows with the Bevanites reached their climax in 1955. In early March the Commons debated the Conservative Government's Defence White Paper. Bevan attacked both the White Paper and the Labour leadership's refusal to condemn it outright: speaking for sixty-three Labour MPs who were to abstain from voting on the party's amendment he said: 'We want from my right hon. friends the leaders of the Opposition an assurance that the language of their amendment does not align the Labour movement behind that recklessness.' By 'that recklessness' Bevan meant what he considered to be the 'war policy' of the Government. Attlee's response was equivocal, and failed to give Bevan the assurance he wanted.

A few days later the shadow cabinet met to decide what action to take against Bevan. Their problem was that Bevan had broken no party rules—even though he had split the party. He had committed a sin rather than a crime. Attlee reluctantly opposed taking any action, even though he had been harmed by the episode more than anyone else; he feared that a worse split might develop if—as some of the hawks wanted—Bevan were to be expelled from the party. But Attlee was overruled by nine votes to four; Callaghan was one of the nine who recommended to the full PLP that the party whip be withdrawn from Bevan.

In a speech on 20 March, Callaghan explained his position: 'The Labour movement would never have reached the peaks and heights of power unless we had been prepared to subordinate our individualism to our Socialism: and it strikes me as very remarkable that some of those who are the best Socialists are the biggest individualists and I find it very difficult to see how you can combine the two . . . We cannot speak with two voices or we are doomed. We cannot have two leaders. We have got to have people who work as a team.'

In the event the party did not split as badly as it might. The whip was withdrawn but, after some nifty footwork by Attlee in the NEC, Bevan was not expelled. At the end of April, in the run-up to the May General Election, the whip was quietly restored to the hero of the left.

1955 was not just a watershed in the Bevanite controversies: it was a watershed for the whole post-war Labour Party. Six months after losing the May General Election, Attlee resigned as leader, and Gaitskell defeated Bevan and Morrison on the first ballot in the PLP election which followed. Now the post-war generation had risen to run the party; and Callaghan—in third place in the shadow cabinet elections—was well placed to advance.

Since 1951 Callaghan had been shadow Transport Minister. Quite apart from his role in the Bevanite arguments he made sure that he stayed in the public eye. His speeches on transport—not normally a subject to raise political passions—were well designed to attract the right kind of attention. At the 1953 party conference, for example, he spoke of 'the narrow South Wales valleys that converge on Cardiff and Newport [where] the railway lines run side by side with part of the great British Election Traction octopus, a private enterprise concern ... The more I discuss and consider this problem, the more I am convinced that it is only through an integrated transport system under public owner-ship that we can solve the needs of the nation.'

While this kind of message succeeded in reaching the party faithful, Callaghan was not neglecting the importance of his wider, public reputation. Television was still a young medium which many politicians treated with disdain. But it was widely viewed, and Callaghan was one of its early political stars. There was only one channel, BBC, and its main political programme was called *In The News*. In April 1954 the Assistant Postmaster-General revealed in answer to a Commons question that Callaghan had appeared on the programme during the previous two years more often than any other politician—thirteen times, out of seventy-five appearances by Labour MPs.

Callaghan was also a regular guest writer when newspapers wanted a Labour view. Here it is possible to see the kind of statements that Callaghan's opponents criticise when they argue that his ideas lack substance. Certainly one *News Chronicle* article during the May 1955 General Election could be compared with the smile of Lewis Carroll's Cheshire cat, for the more you look, the less you see: 'I want a classless society—even though we are going to take longer to get there than I used to think ... I am against a centralised State machine that would control all our affairs. It degenerates into tyranny. On the other hand, I don't want private enterprise to rule the roost—it is irresponsible ...'

Callaghan's stature in the mid 1950s grew, then, not so much because of what in detail he said, but for his ability to *perform*. And, as ever, he was never better than when attacking the Conservatives. One celebrated exchange took place during a debate on the 1956 Suez crisis, after Sir Anthony Eden, then Prime Minister, had ordered British troops to attack Egypt, but before this fact had been officially confirmed. During one rowdy scene Eden shouted angrily across the despatch box at Callaghan: 'You are the master of sitting and shouting. You seldom stand.' Callaghan then climbed to his feet, looked at Eden and said: 'I would like to ask you a question that 50 million people in this country would like to know. Are British troops engaged in Egypt at this moment and where are they?' Eden began to reply: 'Well,

I said yesterday——', but the jeers and boos from the Labour benches prevented his completing his sentence. The exchange was rounded off when Labour MP Reginald Paget asked: 'How can we debate a war when the Government will not tell us whether it has started?' At which point the Speaker, with one of the shafts of wit that punctuate the Commons' most serious debates, said: 'You must do the best you can with the material you have.'

Four weeks later Gaitskell appointed Callaghan shadow Colonial Secretary. The next five years comprised, perhaps, the most unambiguously successful period of Callaghan's front-bench career. It was a time when the last remnants of the British Empire were being wound up, none too successfully, by the Conservatives. This situation was ideally suited to Callaghan's skills: he could vigorously expound Labour policies and attack the Conservatives without risking any dissension in the Labour movement. Indeed, he was now the Labour spokesman on possibly the only subject on which the whole movement was broadly united *and* felt strongly about. His performances were certainly effective, and helped him gain the few thousand extra constituency votes in 1957 that were necessary to elect him to the NEC.

De-colonisation was also a subject which moved Callaghan. Close friends say that *apartheid*, and Conservative policy towards Africa, were things that mattered to him personally, and not just for the political points he could score. His Tory opponents take a different view. One ex-minister recalls how Callaghan was offered the chance to see private government telegrams, in an attempt to maintain a bi-partisan policy. Callaghan consistently refused the offer: 'he preferred to oppose from ignorance', says the ex-minister. (Ironically, the shadow Foreign Secretary was happy to see government telegrams, on a confidential basis. He was none other than Bevan, restored once more to the shadow cabinet.) But one could argue that Callaghan felt so strongly that the Conservatives were wrong in their policies that he did not wish to risk being compromised by having access to selected information which he would not be allowed to use publicly.

Callaghan's speeches from this period show considerable passion. On *Cyprus* (February 1958): 'Men and women are being imprisoned without trial. There is suppression of opinion. Indeed, many of the aspects of the regime which is being con-

ducted in the name of the people of Britain are totalitarian. They
are similar to those which we condemned when they occurred in
Nazi Germany and in Russia. British actions in the last twelve
months have resulted in the British administration being cut off
completely from the people of the island. They are now living in
a small enclave in hostile territory . . .'

On *Nyasaland* (March 1959): 'The deportation of Dr Hastings
Banda [then a nationalist leader, and subsequently Prime
Minister of the country, renamed Malawi] is the crowning folly
of all the Government's blunders in Central Africa . . . Everyone
in the Cabinet, collectively and singly, shares the responsibility
for the unrest which exists in Nyasaland today. We are building
up in Nyasaland a position in which a territory is being forced
into a constitutional path [the ill-fated Central African Federa-
tion] it has no desire to follow and which is contrary to the path
being followed in other parts of Africa.'

On *South Africa* (Labour Party Conference, October 1960):
'Let there be no doubt in anyone's mind that we oppose *apartheid*.
We detest it. Relations between ourselves and the South African
Government cannot improve until they change that policy. It is a
police state. Our own Commonwealth Relations Officer, John
Hatch, cannot get a visa to go there. John Stonehouse was bundled
out in an aircraft, and we all know the story of the Bishop of
Johannesburg [Ambrose Reeves, who had been expelled from
South Africa shortly before the conference]. I am sure they can
bear those minor discomforts; but what about the men and women
who are being torn up from their homes, torn away from their
families and see them no more? What of the men and women now
under arbitrary arrest for committing no crime except calling for
freedom, the rights you enjoy naturally and without a second
thought?'

By 1960 Callaghan could look back on a steady climb up the slopes
of Labour Party politics. With scarcely a setback he had conquered
one foothill after another, at almost regular two- to three-year
intervals: election as an MP; appointment as a junior minister;
election to the shadow cabinet; appointment as shadow Colonial
Secretary; election to the NEC. For much of this time Callaghan
had been considered one of the young, up-and-coming, post-war

generation. But now, in 1960, Callaghan was forty-eight. Labour had just been defeated, in the third successive General Election, and a new bout of left–right arguments was threatening to divide the party.

Callaghan could no longer afford to be a man of promise: he had to become a heavyweight. Both his blooding in the Bevanite battles and his acknowledged debating power helped. But it was following the battles over Gaitskell's leadership in 1960 that Callaghan emerged as one of the party's top four politicians, along with Gaitskell, Wilson and George Brown.

In the aftermath of the 1959 election defeat Labour was divided over two big issues: nationalisation and nuclear disarmament. These divisions reflected a more basic split about the very character of the party—whether it should revert to socialist first principles, or stake out a position as a social democratic party nearer the centre of British politics. As Gaitskell was a firm social democrat, it was inevitable that the arguments of 1960 should focus on him.

Callaghan was an outspoken Gaitskellite throughout. But, as ever, he addressed himself not so much to the issues as to the need for party unity. In January 1960 he said: 'We need the leadership of Hugh Gaitskell who led us so well in the election and whose integrity and courage are beyond question. We cannot afford to waste time on theological arguments about the precise meaning of socialism.' And in June 1960: 'We must ... capitalise our agreements. Play down our divisions. Take the two things on which there are said to be great differences—Clause IV [the nationalisation clause in the Labour Party constitution] and defence. I assert that there is a broad sense of party feeling about both these issues. Our job is to interpret that broad feeling to the nation, not to squabble among each other about every detail of policy.'

Callaghan's strong stand with Gaitskell took some people by surprise. Harold Wilson's private secretary, Marcia Williams (now Lady Falkender) wrote in her book, *Inside Number 10*: 'During the fifties most members of the Labour movement would have supposed Jim Callaghan to be more to the left than the right of the party.' The important point is not that 'most members' (or at any rate a fair number) were wrong, but that they should hold this opinion of Callaghan at all. In any case, the events of 1960 removed all doubts. When Wilson challenged Gaitskell for the party leadership in November 1960, Callaghan publicly supported Gaitskell, who won by 166 votes to 81.

The same month Callaghan stood himself for the deputy leadership, against Brown (another Gaitskellite) and Fred Lee. He announced his decision to stand just two weeks after the Labour Party Conference, at Scarborough, had voted for a policy of unilateral nuclear disarmament, and he specifically stood for the deputy leadership on a platform of rejecting the Scarborough verdict. As Brown was the main candidate of the right, Callaghan did not expect to win. But he polled a creditable 55 votes, and forced the contest to a second ballot which Brown won comfortably. A week later Callaghan's tactics were shown to have paid off. He topped the ballot for the shadow cabinet: Wilson, who had come first the previous year, paid the price of challenging Gaitskell and fell to ninth place.

One year later, Callaghan's loyalty to Gaitskell was rewarded. In a shadow cabinet reshuffle in November 1961, he became shadow Chancellor of the Exchequer. To Callaghan it seemed a passport to one of the most crucial cabinet jobs in a future Labour Government; his position in the party hierarchy was now so secure that he was disappointed but not too dismayed when Anthony Wedgwood Benn edged him off the NEC in the 1962 constituency elections. (Benn had won very considerable support within the Labour movement for his campaign to renounce his peerage and resume his seat in the House of Commons.)

Gaitskell, however, had other ideas. According to very close friends he wanted Callaghan to be *shadow* Chancellor because of his debating skills—but not to be an *actual* Chancellor in a Labour Government, because Callaghan knew too little of economics. Gaitskell planned to give that job to Callaghan's former boss at the Inland Revenue Staff Federation, Douglas Houghton, for a year or two, and then appoint one of Labour's brighter young politicians, Anthony Crosland or Roy Jenkins.

But Gaitskell never had the chance to apply his strategy. In January 1963, after a short illness, he died. From then on Callaghan knew he would have to fight his own party battles.

5

1963–4
Two Battles with
George Brown

'We are redefining and restating our Socialism.'
—HAROLD WILSON, at the 1963 Labour Party Conference

On the evening of Monday 21 January 1963 a group of Gaitskell's closest followers met in Anthony Crosland's Kensington flat: with Crosland were Roy Jenkins's wife Jennifer, the chairman of the TUC General Council Fred Hayday, the Labour Party's Director of Publicity John Harris, and the three leading members of the pro-Gaitskell group Campaign for Democratic Socialism, which had been formed in 1960.

They knew that Wilson would be the left's candidate, and that he would collect some centre votes: since standing against Gaitskell for the party leadership in 1960, Wilson had gone to some lengths to improve his relations with MPs outside the hard left. The problem facing the group in Crosland's flat was, who would stand the best chance of defeating Wilson? George Brown seemed the obvious choice: he had defeated Wilson by 133 votes to 103 just two months earlier in a contest for the deputy leadership. But some people felt that while Brown was well-suited as the party's number two, he was too unpredictable to be chosen as number one. More to the point, Crosland and Harris argued that enough MPs would *think* Brown too unpredictable, and that therefore he would not win.

But who should they choose instead? After discussing such names as Sir Frank Soskice and Michael Stewart, Crosland proposed the name of James Callaghan. The Campaign for Democratic Socialism MPs disagreed: whatever Brown's faults, he was the authentic voice of Gaitskellism, and should be supported. In any case, he was bound to stand.

Confronted with this division on the Labour right, Callaghan faced a difficult choice. If he stood, he would split the anti-Wilson vote or—what would be worse—he would *fail* to split it effectively and end up with such a derisory score that he would lose much of his credibility as one of Labour's leading figures. But if he did not stand, would he not lose credibility anyway? Of the three likely candidates he was the oldest, at fifty: on the 'visiting card' theory of leadership elections (you stand for the leadership one contest before the one you think you can win, and so leave your 'visiting card') it was beyond doubt time to leave his.

For three days Callaghan waited, while two of his colleagues, Denis Healey and Tom Fraser, canvassed MPs' opinions. Three conclusions emerged: first, if both Brown and Callaghan stood, Callaghan would come last and be eliminated after the first ballot; he would, however, pick up enough votes to enhance rather than diminish his credibility. Secondly, some of Callaghan's supporters were so hostile to Brown that even though they disliked the left they would switch their votes to Wilson on the second ballot. Thirdly, if Brown could be persuaded to stand down, Callaghan had a chance of defeating Wilson, for while some of Callaghan's supporters made Wilson their second choice, almost all Brown's supporters (so the Callaghan team thought) would switch to Callaghan.

All these points influenced Callaghan to stand, whatever Brown decided. On Thursday, 24 January Callaghan made a private but formal attempt to persuade Brown to stand down. Brown refused: he did not believe Callaghan's figures; anyway, Brown had fought openly and successfully against the left before, so why should he give up now?

The outcome of the meeting was that both Brown and Callaghan stood against Wilson. Callaghan now for the first time, not only faced MPs as a candidate for the Labour leadership and prospective Prime Minister, but also came under the scrutiny of the media which, in general, had been much kinder to him in earlier years than it normally is to Labour politicians. This time it was different. William Rees-Mogg's opinion in the *Sunday Times* was typical: 'The third man . . . is Mr James Callaghan. Of him it can only be said that he is not of Prime Ministerial calibre. He is the least able of the three men, and, while he was a loyal Gaitskellite, he never took a lonely personal stand on a controversial issue in the party. He may well have political courage; if so, he has not really had the occasion to demonstrate it. That he is a perfectly serious and likeable man, with a favourable television personality, does give him a chance, but does not overcome the objection that he is not up to the job.' Like most of the press Rees-Mogg considered Brown the least objectionable candidate.

But by this time Callaghan had calculated his position carefully. He had some distinguished supporters, including three of his rivals thirteen years later: Healey, Crosland and Jenkins. Douglas Jay and Michael Stewart, both potential cabinet ministers, were also thought to be Callaghan men, along with elder statesmen like George Strauss, Chuter Ede and Reginald Sorenson. The actual ballot, of course, was secret, but these names were certainly on Wilson's private list of Callaghan supporters. And this, to a large extent, was the point. As Crosland confided to a friend at the time: 'If Wilson does get elected on the second ballot, he will know who put him there.'

Callaghan received fewer votes than he hoped, but otherwise the contest went much as he expected. The result of the first ballot was: Wilson 115, Brown 88, Callaghan 41. As Brown's and Callaghan's votes totalled more than Wilson's, there had to be a second ballot, between Wilson and Brown—but Wilson only needed eight of Callaghan's votes to win. Publicly Callaghan displayed no preference, but the Wilson team were confident he would vote for their man. It would clearly make better tactical sense for Callaghan to back the likely winner. In the event the Callaghan vote divided two-to-one for Wilson, who defeated Brown by 144 to 103.

Initially Callaghan seemed to emerge from the contest stronger than Brown. He had shown that he could muster reasonable support among MPs, and Wilson recognised this by keeping him as shadow Chancellor. Brown, however, was refused the post he wanted: shadow Foreign Secretary. What is more, Callaghan now had less to fear from the intellectuals on the Labour right; they might have outflanked him in a Gaitskell Government—but they had no chance of doing so in a Wilson Government. Callaghan could now look forward to being Chancellor in his own right, and not just keeping the seat warm for Crosland or Jenkins.

Callaghan's status was soon challenged by Brown. Within the Labour Party there was a profound distrust of the Treasury, and a desire to have an alternative economic ministry to promote more original and expansionist ideas. As chairman of the Home Policy Committee, Brown ran the most influential sub-committee of the NEC, and so he had an excellent opportunity to guide the party's thinking. The climax was a much-celebrated ride in the back of a taxi in the summer, when Wilson agreed to the idea of a Department of Economic Affairs—with Brown at its head.

Brown lost no time in explaining the exact significance of the decision. Interviewed by Henry Brandon in September 1963 for the *Sunday Times* he said: 'Unless it is absolutely clear that this department is the senior economic department, the top men will still go to the Treasury ... The Treasury will still tend to overlay everything else [other than economic strategy] but the chap who is this Cabinet minister must be the senior economic minister.' The subsequent rise and fall of the DEA is a story of major importance for the whole British economy; and the battles which were fought over its powers and survival go far beyond the personal conflicts between Brown and Callaghan. Nevertheless, part of the story does involve the conflict between the two men, for the idea of the DEA posed a direct, immediate and powerful assault on Callaghan's authority as shadow Chancellor.

Callaghan responded in a more sophisticated but no less public way to Brown's challenge. Two weeks after the *Sunday Times* article, Callaghan 'thought aloud' at a tea party given by the Friends of *Socialist Commentary* during the Labour Party Conference. His remarks were widely reported the next day. Planning, he said, had to be co-ordinated with tax and monetary policies, and with the balance of payments. 'It would be a great mistake to blur responsibilities', he went on; 'the Treasury's role lies clearly in full responsibility for the balance of trade, international liquidity, taxation reform and the strength of sterling.' There is, perhaps, a Jesuitic sense in which this could be deemed consistent with Brown's interview with Brandon. But in effect Callaghan was telling Brown, '*You* may have as many grand ideas as you want, but they will not succeed unless you get your hands on some of the levers of power now controlled by the Treasury. *I* intend making sure you don't.' Callaghan's formal insistence that there was 'no quarrel' between himself and Brown fooled nobody.

It is a measure of Callaghan's political skills (and the Treasury's power) that he not only went on eventually to win this battle, but that he was never in serious danger of losing it, even though Brown's vision of economic policy formation was much more closely tuned to the mood of the Labour Party at that time. 'We are re-defining and we are re-stating our Socialism in terms of the scientific revolution', proclaimed Wilson at the 1963 Party Conference. 'But that revolution cannot become a reality unless we are prepared to make far-reaching changes in economic and social attitudes which permeate our whole society. The Britain that is going to be forged in the white heat of this revolution will be no place for restrictive practices or for outdated methods on either side of industry...' For Callaghan to be talking at the same time about the importance of such conventional things as international liquidity and the strength of sterling may, with hindsight, seem the more prophetic obsession: at the time it sounded simply perverse.

Yet if Callaghan retained his authority in the face of the seductive rhetoric of the 'scientific revolution', he also managed to overcome a more formidable obstacle—his own ignorance of economics.

Despite his experience thirty years earlier in the Inland Revenue, which had led Dalton in 1945 to assume he 'knew something of finance', Callaghan was acutely aware that he lacked a formal economic training. He once recalled an experience as a young MP in the 1945-50 Parliament: 'At first I was dazzled; I'd never heard such marvellous talk before. Then one day I remember listening to Stafford Cripps [who possessed one of Labour's sharpest economic brains] and finding myself thinking "He's wrong, dead wrong." But I couldn't do anything about it—I just couldn't frame the right arguments.'

As shadow Chancellor, Callaghan set about putting this right. In 1959 he had been appointed a visiting fellow of Nuffield

College, Oxford. Nuffield prides itself on forging close links between the academic and political worlds; it is college policy to invite a leading politician from both the Labour and Conservative Parties to serve as visiting fellows. Normally this just involves occasional visits to Oxford to swap ideas and gossip over a dinner at the college's high table. Nuffield's one rule-of-thumb is to keep clear of Oxbridge-reared politicians—so Callaghan was an obvious choice in 1959.

Callaghan used his visiting fellowship more effectively than anyone else. After he was appointed shadow Chancellor by Gaitskell he took a piece of advice offered by Crosland and asked the college to arrange informal, private seminars on economics. For two years, leading up to the 1964 General Election, Labour sympathisers among Oxford's leading economists taught Callaghan the rudiments of economic theory and practice. The main organiser was Ian Little, himself a Nuffield man; other 'tutors' included Thomas Balogh (Balliol), Roger Opie (New College) and a sprinkling of economists from elsewhere, such as Nicholas Kaldor from Cambridge, and Robert Neild and Frank Blackarby of the National Institute of Economic and Social Research in London. Most Friday evenings during term, Callaghan would travel down from London, dine at Nuffield's high table, and afterwards adjourn to one of the don's rooms with some of the economists. (The members of the group would vary from meeting to meeting.) One 'tutor' would read a short paper, while Callaghan scribbled notes. Afterwards there would be a short discussion, with Callaghan asking an occasional question.

Economists who taught Callaghan at this time remember him as a nervous student, extremely conscious of his limitations, trying hard to master a complicated subject from scratch. The seminars did not delve deeply into formal theory, nor did they involve the charts, diagrams or statistics familiar to any orthodox student. They were descriptive, and above all practical, concentrating on following through the consequences of different policy options. Even so, the discussions required a quick mind, and Callaghan showed he had that. 'It was good second or third year undergraduate level, for someone approaching a new subject', says one of Callaghan's tutors: 'My verdict would be that he was worth a good second class degree, but needed to learn more. He was eager—almost pathetically eager.' Another don recalls that 'Callaghan showed a bluff common-sense, and he was quick on the uptake. But I had no impression of any highly incisive mind.' Above all, Callaghan is remembered for being flexible in his approach to policy choices; but when he had made his mind up, he would stick to his decision doggedly. 'He was not all that easy to bamboozle', said one don, echoing Keynes's verdict on the American President Woodrow Wilson: 'but once bamboozled he was impossible to unbamboozle.'

Callaghan's policies as shadow Chancellor were set out with simple clarity in an interview with David Malbert in the London *Evening News* in June 1963. On *taxation*: 'I am in favour of reforming the taxation system. It has fungus on it ... capital gains tax, wealth tax, profits tax—they should all be looked at together from the point of view of rewarding the enterprising and discouraging the passive.' On *nationalising the steel industry*: 'Parliament would have to decide on what terms shareholders would be compensated when the industry is renationalised. But it would be fair.' Callaghan mentioned road transport as another candidate for nationalisation; otherwise 'we have no firm proposals to buy blocks of shares in firms to control their policy'. On *sterling and the balance of payments*: 'We shall not be put off expansion by short-term balance of payments difficulties, unless they are caused by our internal position. We shall avoid stop-go policies and have a steady increase in the level of consumption. We shall seek international co-operation to protect the external value of the pound in its role as a key currency.'

Callaghan's proposals contained rather more bland hope than gritty detail: he told Malbert that he expected the City to respond 'neutrally' to the prospect of a Labour Government. But these were the days of one of Britain's cyclical economic upswings—the beginning of the 'Maudling boom', stimulated by the Conservative Chancellor Reginald Maudling.

Whatever criticisms can be levelled at Callaghan's statements thirteen years ago, they were the statements of a man who was making his mark at last as a political heavyweight. He had established his authority as shadow Chancellor; he was a formidable adversary for Maudling in House of Commons debates; the media were taking him seriously. The fact that he possessed political *gravitas* out of all proportion to his economic competence did not, at the time, seem too important.

As the 1964 election approached, the Maudling boom overheated. Although the magnitude of the coming balance of payments crisis was not known in the summer, Callaghan, Brown and Wilson knew that Labour's economic policies would need revising. Certain basic promises, however, had to be kept. One concerned unemployment; at the 1962 Party Conference, Callaghan had said: '[Our first objective] is that we are unalterable in our determination to maintain full employment.' And a year later, with unemployment just below half a million: 'What a waste of human material and resources!' The second basic promise was to increase pensions and other social benefits. The problem facing the party leadership in the summer of 1964 was how to keep these promises when the balance of payments was so unhealthy.

Even before the election, some of Labour's economic advisers, including Kaldor and Neild, favoured devaluation. Britain's exchange rate had remained constant since 1949; since then the French, Japanese and—most important of all—German economies had been reconstructed, and their exports were penetrating traditional British markets. Kaldor and Neild argued that Britain's economy was now fundamentally threatened by an exchange rate which was too high. Unless the pound were devalued, Britain's exports would be too expensive, its balance of payments would remain unsound, and the Government, especially a Labour Government, would be unable to achieve its domestic economic objectives of rapid growth, full employment and greater public spending.

There were also powerful arguments against devaluation. One was purely political: the previous devaluation had been carried out by a Labour Government, and the party risked being labelled as the 'party of devaluation'. Another argument, which weighed especially heavily with Wilson, was that Labour had a responsibility towards the poorer Commonwealth countries, whose sterling balances would suffer a decline in value. But the third argument was the most substantial—that the weaknesses in the economy did not derive so much from an overvalued pound as from a structurally weak industrial sector. The answer, said the anti-devaluationists, was not to 'featherbed' inefficient companies by allowing them to export at more competitive prices, but to make sure that the right investment went into the right industries.

The detailed arguments, of course, were much more complex than this; and it is important to remember that any *open* discussion of devaluation was considered by the Treasury, the City and the media to verge on treason. The absence of public debate tilted the argument decisively in favour of Wilson, an accomplished economist with clear views, over Callaghan, who was not an economist and held no strong views either way.

Labour's original decision not to devalue—a decision which was to influence profoundly its performance in government—was effectively taken well before the October 1964 General Election. And it was taken by Wilson. The relationship between Callaghan and Wilson over this issue is illustrated by an incident at the Bonnington Hotel in Bloomsbury a few weeks before the election. The hotel was the venue for a series of Labour policy-making meetings, at which a cluster of academics would confer with leading Labour MPs. At the economics meeting, Kaldor spoke strongly in favour of devaluation: instead of maintaining the pound at $2.80, the exchange rate should be cut at least to $2.50. Other economists started to join the debate, when Wilson intervened to cut it short. 'There will be no devaluation', he said firmly; 'you would water the weeds as well as the flowers.' With that, he turned to the next topic.

Callaghan said nothing.

6

1964–6
His Master's Voice

'I always voted at my party's call,
And I never thought of thinking for myself at all.'
—W. S. GILBERT, *HMS Pinafore*

Shortly before 4 p.m. on 16 October 1964 the Queen summoned Harold Wilson to Buckingham Palace and invited him to form a Government. After thirteen years in opposition, Labour had won a narrow General Election vicotry, with an overall Commons majority of four seats. Wilson immediately started recruiting colleagues for his Cabinet. George Brown was his first appointment, First Secretary of State—that is, deputy Prime Minister—and Secretary of State for Economic Affairs. Callaghan's appointment as Chancellor of the Exchequer came two hours later. Thus, with protocol carefully maintained, Wilson confirmed his divide-and-rule approach to economic policy making. Brown was given the status; Callaghan, with the Treasury behind him, was given the power.

The first few hours of the Labour Government established more than status: it also determined the economic strategy of the next three years. On reaching their new offices—Brown at 5 p.m., Callaghan at 7 p.m.—the two Ministers received identical Treasury briefs. Their subject was the balance of payments, and they contained a new forecast for the year's deficit: £800 million. Worse still, the briefs pointed out that the deficit was deteriorating so that when the Conservatives left office it was running at a *rate* of no less than £1,000 million a year. This was worse than anything Wilson, Brown or Callaghan had expected, even though Labour had sharply attacked Conservative economic policy during the run-up to the election. As Wilson, recalling a remark by John Kennedy, said when asked what his greatest shock was on coming to power: 'It was to discover that everything we'd said about our opponents was true.' Briefly, the option of devaluation was again discussed. Attached to the Treasury's analysis of the balance of payments (which had been drafted by one of its brightest young officials, Callaghan's son-in-law Peter Jay) was an appendix setting out the case for devaluation, and the case against. Formally the appendix presented the arguments neutrally, in a purely factual way; but it had been prepared by the the the Bank of England, which was opposed to devaluation, so the appendix conveyed no great enthusiasm for altering the exchange rate.

In any case there was never much chance that the Government would devalue. When Wilson, Brown and Callaghan met the next day, Wilson immediately announced that he opposed devaluation. He quickly convinced Brown, but Callaghan wanted to avoid a hasty decision. After a brief discussion, however, Callaghan acquiesced: there would be no devaluation. By the end of the day all three men agreed that the pound would be defended to the very end; not only that—they agreed that there should be no discussion of it inside government. On the rare occasions when Treasury officials discussed it afterwards, they referred to devaluation as 'the unmentionable'—and even, on occasions, 'British Rail'. Wilson's argument for banning discussion was that the smallest news leak, or softest whisper, that devaluation was even being contemplated, would in itself cause such a run on the pound as to make devaluation inevitable.

Robert Neild—one of the pro-devaluation economists brought into the Treasury as an adviser—made one serious attempt a few days later to overturn the 'no discussion' ruling. One evening he visited Sir William Armstrong, then Joint Permanent Secretary to the Treasury, at Sir William's flat in Westminster and told him that discussion of devaluation must be allowed. It remained, he said, a policy option even if it had been ruled out for the moment; one day the Government might choose—or be forced—to change its mind, and it would be ludicrous to reach that situation unprepared. Armstrong, a small, neat man who looked the very model of a modern Treasury mandarin, sat in his oversized chair with his feet barely touching the ground, and said coldly that the

Prime Minister's ruling must be obeyed. Neild persisted. The meeting finally ended three hours later with Armstrong, shoes off, standing in front of the fire giving Neild an extempore lecture on the interaction of politics, government and economics. Neild sat, open-mouthed and thoroughly defeated.

Subsequently occasional attempts were made, by Neild and others, to reopen the subject, but they never got very far. In the spring of 1965 a group of economic advisers signed a memorandum demanding devaluation; Wilson personally ordered its suppression. In March 1966 another attempt was made to raise the issue; this time Wilson ordered all copies of the offending document to be destroyed. Callaghan was aware throughout that there was a devaluation lobby; but even when distinguished outsiders suggested it to him, as Emile van Lennap, chairman of the European Economic Community Monetary Commission, did in November 1964, Callaghan replied simply and briefly that it was not on. Wilson determined the policy, but Callaghan was an unquestioning lieutenant.

With devaluation ruled out, Callaghan had the responsibility for devising an alternative policy for correcting the balance of payments. The story of the next three years is the story of his—and the whole Government's—failure to find a policy that would work. Samuel Brittan expressed it succinctly in *Steering the Economy*: 'If the Prime Minister's mind was closed to argument on the exchange rate, irrespective of any new facts and figures which might be produced, his best course would have been to have deflated in October 1964, and then proceeded to run the economy at a higher margin of unemployment ... The really serious mistake of the Labour Government, after both the 1964 and 1966 elections, was to refuse to admit that a choice between devaluation and relying on unaccompanied deflation had become necessary.'

On 26 October 1964, ten days after becoming Chancellor, Callaghan unveiled his first set of measures to the Commons. Revealing for the first time in public the size of the balance of payments deficit, he announced that there would be a temporary surcharge of 15 per cent on all imports, except food and raw materials, and an average 2 per cent subsidy for exports, in the form of tax rebates. The mechanics for these measures had been prepared while Maudling had been Chancellor: hence Callaghan's ability to announce them so quickly. (Indeed, Maudling himself commented at the time that Callaghan had inherited 'our problems and our remedies'.)

Callaghan believed that this direct action on Britain's trade would go sufficiently far towards closing the deficit so that he would not need to restrain the domestic economy. He went out of his way to say that 'the Government reject entirely deflation or "stop-and-go", which inflicted incalculable damage on our industrial system from 1951 onwards, with the creation of substantial unemployment. We have decided on alternative ways [of correcting the balance of payments].'

One trouble with these 'alternative ways' was that foreigners did not like them. Britain was accused of breaking the rules of the General Agreement on Tariffs and Trade. The Organisation for Economic Co-operation and Development (OECD) censured the Government. Only the American administration approved Callaghan's package. And meanwhile sterling faced growing pressure: on 3 November alone, the official gold reserves fell by £31 million to £876 million, the lowest for three years.

Worse was to come. On 11 November Callaghan introduced an autumn Budget. It carried out Labour's manifesto promises to raise pensions and abolish NHS prescription charges. To pay for these, he raised the standard rate of income tax by 6d, and increased the duty on petrol. In fact, the Budget was slightly deflationary, but in presenting it Callaghan managed to obscure this point: it would have been music in the ears of foreign bankers, but to the Labour Party it would have sounded more like a bugle playing the retreat. As it was, holders of sterling regarded the Budget as extravagantly doctrinaire.

But the real damage was done not by any of the actual Budget measures so much as by what Callaghan said he intended to do the following year—introduce corporation and capital gains tax. The taxes, though naturally unpopular in the City, were eminently defensible measures; but Callaghan did not say how they would work, or what rates he intended. So the City and overseas bankers reacted as anyone would who knew that something nasty was going to happen, but did not know exactly what it was or how nasty it would be. They panicked. Sterling continued to leave the country and pressure mounted for the Government to raise the Bank Rate.

Callaghan left Wilson to try to convince the City that a Labour Government would stand by the pound. On Monday, 16 November the Prime Minister spoke at a Guildhall dinner: 'I want to take this opportunity tonight, in the heart of this financial centre, to proclaim not only our faith but our determination to keep sterling strong and to see it riding high ... If anyone, at home or abroad, doubts the firmness of that resolve and acts upon their doubts, let them be prepared to pay the price for their lack of faith in Britain.' It was Dunkirk Wilson at his bulldog best. But it did not work.

When sterling is weak, but the Prime Minister says he will preserve its value, it is taken universally as a sign that the Bank Rate (today the minimum lending rate) is to be raised, so that London's higher interest rates will attract money back to the City. After Wilson's speech, the financial community waited expectantly for an announcement the following Thursday—the traditional day for changing the Bank Rate.

The Cabinet debated what to do. A 2 per cent rise to 7 per cent would make the pound highly attractive again—but at the same time could be interpreted as a panic move. A 1 per cent increase would be a more sober response, but would it be enough? And there was another consideration: raising the Bank Rate meant raising the level of almost all domestic interest rates, and this would discourage industry from borrowing money for investment. George Brown, as the expansionist Secretary for Economic Affairs, fought hard against any rise; moreover, he had a tactical advantage in that he presided over the first Cabinet meeting, on Tuesday, 17 November, to discuss the issue. (Wilson had gone to Lancaster University to receive an honorary degree.)

By contrast, Callaghan was undecided; just as he had urged delaying a decision on devaluation one month earlier, he wanted now to postpone a decision on the Bank Rate. There was, perhaps, one way out: Wilson could contact America's President Johnson and ask for a loan to help Britain until the crisis passed. The next day, Wednesday, Wilson sent Johnson a telegram requesting a loan, and hoping for a decision before Thursday morning, when the Bank Rate decision would have to be made.

Johnson waited a few hours too long. By Thursday lunchtime Wilson and Callaghan had not heard from him; but while they waited they agreed not to raise the Bank Rate. When Johnson's reply did arrive during the afternoon, it was non-committal. And by now, the financial markets were dumbfounded: no Bank Rate rise, no loan, just Monday's rhetorical flourish by Wilson. The reserves fell another £20 million during the day, and shares slid.

On Friday evening, 20 November, while other ministers were at Chequers for a weekend gathering which had been planned for some time, Callaghan had a long session with Lord Cromer, the Governor of the Bank of England. Cromer reported to Callaghan that once more the reserves had fallen, and urged that Bank Rate should be raised as soon as possible—not waiting even until the following Thursday. Callaghan, who had staggered through the week in a state of indecision, was convinced, and travelled to Chequers to persuade Wilson and Brown.

It was one of the most tortured weekends of the whole Labour Government. Ministers, short of sleep, knew that they had no more room for the kind of error they had made in not raising the Bank Rate already. But the more this point sank home, the more prone some ministers were to erratic responses. George Brown completely reversed his previous opposition to even a 1 per cent rise in Bank Rate: he now argued that the crisis had grown so serious that a 2 per cent increase should be announced as soon as the money markets opened the next Monday. Callaghan's reaction was even more cataclysmic. According to Lord Wigg, then Paymaster General, in his memoirs: 'Jim Callaghan's lips quivered, his hands shook, he had no idea what had hit him ... I remember vividly Callaghan mumbling, "We can't go on. We shall have to devalue."'

Eventually Wilson, Callaghan and Brown did agree to raise the rate by 2 per cent, and Callaghan returned to London to make the arrangements. He remained in a state of some shock. Richard Crossman, in *The Diaries of a Cabinet Minister*, recorded being asked round to the Chancellor's office at 11 Downing Street early on the Monday morning: 'There was Callaghan, heavy and gloomy as ever. "I am the Selwyn Lloyd", he said, "of this Government." He was obviously over-awed by the situation and full of self-pity.' (There has been some controversy over the accuracy of the Crossman diaries. But Treasury officials and advisers from that time say that the references to Callaghan and the Treasury were broadly correct.)

After the Bank Rate had been raised, it soon became apparent that the move had failed: the Bank of England reported 'massive and growing' sales of sterling. So in the event, the 'crisis' psychology induced by announcing an unusually large rise on an unusual day proved more telling than any objective advantage the new Bank Rate offered for holders of sterling. When Callaghan appeared in the House of Commons on the Monday afternoon, the Conservative shadow Chancellor Reginald Maudling gave him a rough ride: 'The speculative movements', said Maudling, 'both by their nature and timing clearly derive from the recent action of the Government, including, in particular, the Budget, the taxation proposals and the inept handling of the [import] surcharge.' Maudling's attack was the more powerful for being well justified: whatever the merits of the Government's economic strategy, its tactics were extremely inadequate.

Finally the pound was saved by a $3 billion loan arranged by eleven central banks; after the announcement on Wednesday evening, 25 November, Callaghan could begin to face the House of Commons with some confidence once more. 'This concerted action of the monetary authorities of the western world', he told MPs the next day, 'will demonstrate to those who have been influenced by rumours about the future of sterling that their fears are groundless.' Sterling started to stabilise, and though little money actually returned to London, the outflow was greatly reduced. For the time being, the crisis had passed.

This episode has a strange sequel. In March 1966 the *Sunday Times* published two long articles by Henry Brandon called 'How Sterling Came in from the Cold'. They described in great detail the financial crisis of November 1964, in the context of Labour's troubled first year in office. What was not revealed at the time of the articles (later expanded into the book *In the Red*) was the great concern they caused Wilson and Callaghan—to the point where Callaghan tried to persuade the *Sunday Times* to defer publication.

The crux of the problem was that the articles were about to appear, when Wilson called a General Election. By this time Sir William Armstrong at the Treasury had read a first draft, and recorded in a file note his professional respect for Brandon ('He seems to have made a serious attempt to be balanced ... He naturally was evasive about his sources.'). Armstrong's note says that Brandon agreed to correct a few factual errors; otherwise the only substantial point on which Brandon was swayed was that he agreed to omit the names of four economic advisers who favoured devaluation (Kaldor, Neild, Balogh and Sir Donald MacDougall). There were aspects of Brandon's articles Armstrong did not like: 'I thought they gave an unfair impression of the Government being buffeted about by events and the initiatives always being taken by somebody else—the Americans, the Governor of the Bank of England or the Continental Central Bankers.' Armstrong's final conclusion, however, was clear: 'I did not feel myself ... that the [articles were] so damaging that I must plead with him not to publish [them].'

Derek Mitchell, in Wilson's private office, took a similar line on the articles. In a note to Wilson on 3 March 1966 he wrote: 'I do not myself believe that they will have a damaging effect on confidence. On the contrary they may give the impression (which could be damaging from another point of view) that the Labour Government leant over a little too far backwards to appease foreign opinion, including, of course, American opinion.'

On whether to take action, Mitchell posed two choices: 'One, which the Chancellor had in his mind, was to persuade Lord Thomson to withhold the articles at any rate until after the Election. On this I would only say that it would be highly damaging if it became known that the Chancellor had got the articles suppressed. Although it could be said that this had been done in the interests of sterling, it would be assumed that it had been done in the interests of the Labour Party during an Election campaign ... The second would be to see Henry Brandon yourself. Ostensibly this would be so that you could give him your own account of some critical events ... This would improve still more the presentation of your own role, though inevitably at the expense of depressing that of the Chancellor . . . This is an awkward situation, but in retrospect I do not think that there is anything that could have been done by HMG to avoid it (apart from strangling the project at birth, which would have been exceedingly difficult).'

At the end of his note Mitchell added a postscript which showed that Callaghan had taken things into his own hands: 'Since dictating this I have heard that following your talk with the Chancellor this afternoon he has asked Lord Thomson to defer (or cancel?) publication and will be seeing him and Denis Hamilton [then editor of the *Sunday Times*] early tomorrow morning. If the *Sunday Times* give way all well and good. I would only emphasise the risk of a leak . . .'

At 8.30 the next morning, Friday, 4 March, Lord Thomson and Denis Hamilton arrived at 11 Downing Street to listen to Callaghan's appeal. With them in the Chancellor's office were Ian Bancroft, Callaghan's private secretary, and Armstrong. Callaghan told Thomson and Hamilton that the foreign exchange markets were jittery, and the articles could damage sterling. Hamilton replied that this seemed unlikely as the articles did not pinpoint serious blame on anyone, and in any case they were purely historical. Lord Thomson listened in silence: he held to a firm rule that as proprietor of the *Sunday Times* he never interfered in matters of editorial judgement. But after a while he did intervene to make one point. Looking at Armstrong, Thomson asked: 'Do *you* think the articles will harm sterling?' Armstrong was in a difficult position: only two weeks earlier he had told Brandon that the articles were *not* likely to damage the pound seriously. He fidgeted in his chair, and after a few seconds replied carefully: 'I don't think they will do it any good.' Neither Callaghan nor Armstrong could point to any factual errors in the articles.

Hamilton left the meeting promising to reconsider publication, but warning Callaghan that he would almost certainly go ahead. Later that day he telephoned Callaghan to confirm that the first article would be published, as planned, the following Sunday. Luckily for the Government, though, Derek Mitchell's fears were not realised, for there was no leak of what Callaghan had done. But the time spent by Wilson, Callaghan and senior civil servants considering the articles indicates how sensitive they felt about the Government's handling of sterling.

After the November 1964 crisis Callaghan continued to show signs of strain as Chancellor. Treasury colleagues recall that he worked prodigiously hard, 'trying desperately to keep up', as one official put it. He would stay in his office until late at night going through his papers, attempting to master the rapidly changing circumstances of a subject he knew too little about. Crossman's diary entry for 14 December 1964 said of Callaghan: 'There is a man who simply isn't enthralled and stimulated and excited by the challenge of his office. He feels unhappy and insecure, and I sometimes suspect that he feels he has been hoicked up above his level and given a job which he has no taste for because he feels he can't get on top of it.'

There was just one thing going for Callaghan. If the problems of sterling worried him, they crippled George Brown. Brown's ambitious plans for a 4 per cent economic growth rate became more and more unreal, and with each successive tremor on the world's money markets, Brown's Department of Economic Affairs lost a little more of its credibility and influence. Brown subsequently wrote: 'We were given the long-term planning but we were not given the short-term control ... As a result the [Treasury] knights succeeded in re-establishing their effective final control. Traditional methods of money-management, both internal and external, remained the ultimate sanction, and we were kept in the old straitjacket because overseas confidence was always held to be paramount and it was repeatedly claimed to be achievable only by deflation.'

The long retreat into Government-by-deflation gathered pace after the Bank Rate crisis. On 8 December 1964 Callaghan told the clearing banks to slow down their rate of growth of lending. On 15 December he announced that he was abandoning his plans for a wealth tax. As the months passed, it became steadily more obvious that the plans drawn up by the Labour leadership before taking office would not be fulfilled for some years.

A Cabinet meeting on 11 February 1965 provided a vivid illustration of the pressures facing the Government. Crossman, as Housing Minister, proposed a modest expansion of the council

c

house building programme. He recorded in his diary that 'I was followed by Callaghan who in a long, violent harangue said that we were going to crack up and crash unless the increase in public expenditure could be halted.' Another minister recalled Callaghan saying: 'If we go on like this, we shall slide into catastrophe. Every extra item of social expenditure is noted by the bankers who have lent us money. They do not hesitate to write in and tell me.' Eventually, with Wilson's support, Crossman got his way. But more normally Callaghan got his way, and carried out his regular task of introducing distasteful measures.

The April 1965 Budget is an example of this: Callaghan spoke against a background of a weak pound (the $3 billion loan had recently had to be renewed), and forecasts of the balance of payments remaining seriously in deficit through both 1965 and 1966. The Budget measures included higher drink and tobacco duties, capital gains tax, and a variety of other measures, designed to deflate the economy by £250 million a year. This was not a large amount, but it did enable the Conservatives to mount an effective attack against Labour: 'The Budget soaks the rich', said Edward Heath in the Commons; 'it also soaks the poor. It is nasty, brutish and long.' Callaghan's troubles were heightened by the tiny size of Labour's majority, now down to two following a by-election defeat at Leyton. In the debates that followed, 1,222 amendments were tabled, of which 440 came from the Government. Three times Labour was defeated, including one notorious occasion when a group of Tory MPs 'ambushed' the Government by calling for a division in the middle of the night when a number of Labour MPs had gone home. It was the first Finance Bill for forty-one years in which the Government had ever lost a vote; and according to ministerial colleagues of that time Callaghan was badly bruised by the experience.

The Budget's central failing, however, had nothing to do with any of the Conservative amendments; it was simply not deflationary enough. Crossman recorded discussing the matter with Kaldor in early May: 'Not having devalued,' said Nicky [Kaldor], 'we mustn't have any illusions. We shall have to go through a long period of savage deflation and mass unemployment.' The problem was exacerbated by the fact that the tighter credit and deflation from the previous winter seemed to be having no impact:

unemployment remained at an extremely low 1·2 per cent, and the trade deficit remained disturbingly wide.

By late July 1965, Callaghan decided that further action was needed. He advised the Cabinet to support a new deflationary package, with tighter hire purchase restrictions and the postponement of some public spending projects. Crossman recorded the fierce debate which took place in the Cabinet on 27 July, with Crossman, Roy Jenkins and Anthony Crosland arguing that Callaghan's strategy was misguided and inadequate. What Crossman omitted was the fact that the subject of devaluation was briefly raised at this meeting—more than a year earlier than the date generally given for the first airing of devaluation inside the Cabinet. Barbara Castle said that those who had advocated devaluation in October 1964 were right; we should devalue now, she said, instead of surrendering the Labour Government to Tory policies. Crosland later told friends that he too favoured devaluation then—but felt bound by a private undertaking he had given Callaghan not to press the point in Cabinet. In the event, the Cabinet approved the package, even though it included, in Crossman's words, 'the abandonment of so many promises and pledges'. Callaghan presented it to the Commons the same afternoon.

At a Cabinet meeting the following week, on 3 August, ministers continued to argue about the precise application of the spending cuts Callaghan had announced. Crosland said his long-term plans for education had been wrecked; Crossman complained that he was still in dispute with the Treasury on housing expenditure. Callaghan shouted at them: 'If you all go on like this, I shall resign. I warn you, I'm not prepared to take much more.'

A few weeks later George Brown introduced the National Plan, which still enshrined his cherished 4 per cent growth target. But even as it was published, it was assumed to be, at best, a blueprint for some future occasion, and at worst, still-born. In its August 1965 review, the National Institute for Economic and Social Research observed that Callaghan's measures should correct the balance of payments 'at the cost of slowing down the rise in national output nearly to a stop'. Callaghan indicated what the purpose of the whole exercise had been when he told the 1965 Labour Party Conference: 'We have had a tremendous battle over the last 12 months. We have to some extent come through it. Sterling is safe—that battle is won.'

In private, Callaghan justified his defence of sterling by arguing that whatever its *economic* merits, devaluation was politically suicidal: 'Even Treasury officials are alarmed at the damage to Labour which devaluation would cause', he said on one occasion. 'It would set democracy in this country back for years.'

Over the next few months something odd happened. The balance of payments did improve—as expected—but despite the Government's measures, unemployment stayed stubbornly low, and economic growth continued at 2 to 2·5 per cent a year. In the first quarter of 1966, personal disposable income was more than 6 per cent higher than a year earlier, even after taking inflation into account. The Government took advantage of this situation to hold a General Election; this time Labour returned to power with a Commons majority of 97.

According to Crossman, Callaghan had said shortly before the election that he wanted to move from the Exchequer. It would certainly have been a good time to do so, for Callaghan could claim, on the surface, to have returned the economy to something approaching good health. He was, for example, able to tell the Commons on 1 March that one of Britain's important debts—to the Federal Reserve Bank—had been repaid.

But Wilson kept Callaghan as Chancellor; and the improvement in the economy which had helped Labour win the election proved (in Samuel Brittan's words) to have been the Government's 'first false dawn'. Callaghan was still in charge at the Treasury when the fat hit the fire.

The origins of the July 1966 sterling crisis are disputed. According to Wilson, in *The Labour Government 1964–70*, 'it hit us with incredible rapidity. On Friday 1 July, Jim Callaghan and I met to discuss the economic situation ... The Chancellor, with all his Treasury and Bank of England briefs before him, drew a picture of blue skies in every direction ... Then came the publication on July 4 of the June gold figures showing a further drain on sterling ... Within a week the Chancellor's hopes were dashed.' Wilson blamed foreign speculators, who reacted to the two-month strike of the National Union of Seamen—or rather to the *consequences* of the strike, which had been settled at the end of June.

A private Treasury briefing paper for ministers, written later in the year, gave a different account. It started by conceding that there had been 'a crisis of confidence in sterling' but went on to say that 'it would be wrong to view the measures [taken on 20 July] as occasioned solely by speculative pressures on the pound. They also reflected the fact that it had become clear to the Government that the balance of payments was not improving as rapidly as had been expected. The measures were necessary, that is to say, in order to accelerate the process of eliminating the deficit and replacing it with the surplus needed to repay the heavy short-term borrowing of recent years.'

Crossman's account is more consistent with the Treasury than with Wilson. He wrote as early as 26 May 1966: 'I think we are moving towards another Government Crisis.' The Budget had gone down badly—notably Callaghan's controversial proposal for Selective Employment Tax—and the pound was in trouble. On 13 June, at a Cabinet Housing Committee, Crossman heard that public expenditure would have to be cut back further; and at a 21 June meeting of the Cabinet, Crossman recorded that 'Harold's leadership was a bit shaken because we were coming into the open with our anxieties about the whole economic situation'.

If the origins of the crisis are disputed, the date when it exploded in Cabinet is not. On 12 July Callaghan circulated in Cabinet a document admitting that his deflationary measures had failed to hold back consumption sufficiently, and public expenditure would need to be reduced by an additional £500 million. The eight days that followed—culminating in the measures announced in the Commons on 20 July—were the most fraught of the Labour Government, with the possible exception of the November 1964 Bank Rate crisis. Drawing on the published accounts of ministers, as well as on the private recollections of people closely involved, it is possible to piece together an account of what happened. It shows Callaghan up in a rather different light from the way he is conventionally portrayed.

The immediate response of the Cabinet to Callaghan's document was shock. Crosland, the Education Secretary, and Crossman,

Minister of Housing, both opposed the cuts, arguing that it was the function of a Labour Government to protect public spending. 'At this point', wrote Crossman, 'the Chancellor woke up and said that he must tell Cabinet frankly that he didn't know how we were going to get out of the mess. We had totally failed to reach our objectives, we were drifting into devaluation in the worst possible conditions and he didn't know how he could retain his position as Chancellor.' The Cabinet meeting ended inconclusively, with Brown also lined up with those who opposed the cuts.

The following morning, 13 July, Callaghan called two men into his office at 11 Downing Street: Kaldor, the adviser who had favoured devaluation all along, and Ian Bancroft, Callaghan's private secretary. Callaghan said: 'I've got something to tell you. I've decided we'll have to devalue.' Callaghan had been struck by the extent of the opposition in Cabinet to further public spending cuts; his political antennae also told him that the cuts would be unpopular with Labour MPs and with the party outside Parliament. The only alternative was devaluation.

Two interpretations can be placed on what happened next. The first is that Callaghan made a serious, but short-lived, attempt to persuade Wilson to devalue. The second is that Callaghan deployed his tactical skills to the full and, knowing that Wilson would rule out devaluation, sought to prevent the odium for cuts and other unpopular measures from falling entirely on his own shoulders.

Callaghan certainly asked a tiny group of Treasury officials to prepare contingency plans for a devaluation on 31 July—'D-day'. But according to one man extremely close to Callaghan, 'Jim is *never* in favour of something impractical. Wilson's opposition made devaluation impractical, so Jim knew that it would only happen if it were forced on the Government by events.' This suggests that the 'contingency' in the 31 July planning was not a change of heart by the Prime Minister, but an unstoppable run on sterling.

After seeing Kaldor and Bancroft, Callaghan contacted Brown. The two men agreed to press Wilson jointly to devalue rather than deflate. (Wilson's account is that 'on my return [from Sussex University] I found a difficult situation had arisen ... I heard that under George's pressure Jim Callaghan was weakening [over devaluation].') That Wednesday evening, Wilson summoned Callaghan next door to 10 Downing Street. At the end of the meeting Callaghan withdrew his request for devaluation; in return Wilson agreed to announce the Government's new economic measures to the Commons himself. This meant that Wilson would also have the chief responsibility for holding the Cabinet in line, as well as for facing criticisms in the party and among the public. If it was Callaghan's objective to shift responsibility in this way, he succeeded totally.

At the same time, Callaghan was once more in disagreement with Brown, who continued to favour devaluation throughout the crisis. The following morning, Thursday, 14 July, Wilson told the Cabinet that because of this disagreement, he would make a holding statement to the Commons in the afternoon. When Wilson did speak to MPs he was unspecific about actual measures: 'I intend to make a further statement in the House in the near future about the measures we shall propose, which will have the effect of providing the restraint that is necessary ... [including] a substantial reduction in overseas Government expenditure.'

The 'further statement' was fixed for the next Wednesday, 20 July. But during the intervening week Wilson had to go to Moscow: he had arranged his visit to the Soviet leaders some weeks earlier, and to postpone it now would create the kind of crisis atmosphere he wanted to avoid. His absence from London for three crucial days, however, gave other ministers an opportunity to lobby behind his back. Wilson insists in his memoirs that 'there was no plot, no conspiracy, no cabal, no organization'; yet Crossman's diaries have already revealed that on Monday and Tuesday, 18 and 19 July, some intensive discussions took place among senior ministers to marshal arguments in Cabinet in favour of devaluing or floating the pound, instead of deflating the economy.

Crossman's account is incomplete. It is possible, in fact, to trace the origins of the attempt to force devaluation through Cabinet even earlier—to the previous Friday, 15 July. While Wilson prepared to fly to Moscow on the Saturday morning, Brown was in Durham for the miners' gala. During the Friday evening he contacted most of the Cabinet by telephone and marked down five, apart from himself, in favour of devaluation or floating: Crosland and Roy Jenkins from the Labour right, and Crossman, Tony Benn and Barbara Castle from the left. It seems that Brown's style did not altogether please his supporters on this issue, for Jenkins told Callaghan the following morning that Brown had sounded 'hysterical' over the telephone, and he, Jenkins, had been unable to make much sense of the conversation.

Even so, Callaghan understood well enough that there would be strong minority resistance to the public spending cuts when they came to be discussed in detail. So he continued to tell ministerial colleagues in private that devaluation would be inevitable sooner or later: 'We cannot go on staggering from crisis to crisis', his argument ran, 'for if we get help from Washington it will only be by way of loans which means, in practice, buying a few months' breathing space.' Callaghan proposed that if devaluation were completely ruled out for the immediate future, then American support for the pound, together with the public spending cuts, should be specifically linked to a plan to float or devalue the pound in the spring of 1967.

Wilson knew that this was Callaghan's view; but the furthest he would go when the Cabinet met on Tuesday evening, 19 July, to settle the detailed cuts, was to promise that if unemployment rose significantly above half a million he would 'consider' devaluation.

On Wednesday afternoon, 20 July, Wilson announced the measures to the Commons. They included tougher hire purchase restrictions, higher duties on petrol and alcohol, a rise in purchase tax, a cut-back in public investment and military spending abroad, a six-month freeze on prices and incomes, and a £50 limit on the amount of foreign currency tourists could take abroad.

George Brown's reaction was the best publicised: he resigned—and then withdrew his resignation. Brown described in his memoirs the pressures on him to stay in the Cabinet: 'The most telling argument put to me was that if I resigned I should have to say why I resigned, and if I said that the Government was seriously split on whether or not to devalue, there would at once be a most devastating run on our reserves.' Three weeks later, however, Wilson gave Brown a new job, that of Foreign Secretary.

Callaghan's role received far less attention at the time. With hindsight he is seen to have been politically more skilful than ever before, and also to have grasped the problem of sterling's weakness better, and earlier, than he is generally given credit for. He had emerged from the July crisis with a string of tactical victories: Wilson, not Callaghan, had made the unpopular announcement; Callaghan's stature in the eyes of colleagues had survived better than Brown's erratic behaviour; and with Brown's move to the Foreign Office, the four-year battle between the two men for control over economic policy had been finally, decisively, settled in Callaghan's favour. Yet one important criticism remains. If Callaghan displayed considerable strategic foresight, he also showed extreme tactical cynicism, for the evidence suggests that he deployed his views on sterling more to secure short-term political advantage than to correct a government policy he knew to be inadequate.

7

1966-7: Devaluation

There is no good in arguing with the inevitable. The only argument available with an east wind is to put on your overcoat.'
—JAMES RUSSELL LOWELL

Samuel Brittan describes the winter and spring of 1966-7 as the Labour Government's 'second false dawn'. (The first one had begun in the autumn of 1965 and collapsed in July 1966.) Britain's debts to the foreign central banks were repaid; deflation—for once—did take place as intended; and the balance of payments improved. In keeping with a well-established tradition, Callaghan wrote a New Year message which the *Financial Times* published on 31 December 1966: 'The Government's major objective continues to be economic recovery and 1967 will therefore see a working out of existing policies rather than any dramatic new changes ... Our aim will be expansion without inflation ... The Government's long-term objectives continue to be based on a viable balance of payments, full employment and an expanding economy.' The same optimism appeared in the 1967 spring Budget. Under the slogan 'steady as she goes', Callaghan predicted a balance of payments 'surplus in 1967 as a whole with an even bigger one in 1968'. He forecast that the economic growth rate would be a sustained and, by British standards, creditable 3 per cent; unemployment would be held down at 2 per cent. In June 1967, Callaghan spoke even more buoyantly: 'The period of standstill is finished. During the next twelve months there will be a gentle but progressive improvement in the standard of life of every family in the country ... We are now beginning on a period of controlled growth and expansion.'

There are a number of reasons why these hopes were shattered by devaluation in November 1967. (One of the best economic analyses can be found in Brittan's *Steering the Economy*.) In part, British exports suffered from a simultaneous recession in the

United States and Germany; in part Britain's economy (like that of most countries) suffered from the closure of the Suez Canal after the six-day Middle East War in June. And in defence of Callaghan it should also be mentioned that he had not been alone in the spring in anticipating economic recovery: the independent National Institute for Economic and Social Research shared his optimism. Nevertheless, the symptoms of malaise were visible long before the last hectic days which finally provoked devaluation.

These symptoms first started to appear in May. On 2 May, Wilson announced that Britain would seek membership of the European Economic Community—four years after General de Gaulle's veto of the Macmillan Government's application. Common Market officials soon pointed out that the value of the pound, and the role of sterling as a reserve currency, would have to be called into question. And as if to underline the point, the April trade figures—published in May—were the worst for many months. This is the time when Treasury officials began to see some merit in devaluation.

By the summer the Government knew it could not keep its pledge on unemployment: the highest summer figures since 1950 were recorded, and the number out of work was expected to approach three-quarters of a million in the coming winter. There could now be little doubt that it would be impossible both to stabilise the balance of payments and to bring down unemployment without devaluation. But in public Callaghan firmly rejected this argument. 'Those who advocate devaluation', he told MPs in July 1967, 'are calling for a reduction in the wage levels and the wage standards of every member of the working class of this country. Devaluation is not the way out of Britain's difficulties.' Instead, Callaghan trusted to wage and price restraint to restore the economy. When he appeared at the Labour Party Conference in Scarborough that autumn he built his defence of government economic policy around a vigorous denunciation of trade unionists who demanded a return to free collective bargaining: 'This is life, and we have got to face up to it. Reflect before you support a resolution which calls for a return to a free-for-all, because if we do return to a free-for-all we know the consequences—inflation.' Callaghan's speech worked triumphantly: it received the loudest ovation of the conference, and succeeded in swaying the majority of delegates behind government policy.

But as we have seen, Callaghan's public defence of government policy masked serious private doubts which he had held for more than a year. In late October came the news that finally set the Cabinet on course for devaluation; Britain's gold and foreign exchange reserves were dwindling again—and the Treasury had revised its forecasts to show that Britain's balance of payments would end up massively in deficit in both 1967 and 1968. The optimism of the spring had finally evaporated.

The devaluation operation was carried out faultlessly. Over eight days, leading up to the announcement on 18 November, detailed preparations were made and foreign central banks consulted in great secrecy.

Callaghan and Wilson concealed their devaluation plans from the Cabinet until 16 November, two days before the public announcement. On 14 November—four days after the Treasury had set the machinery in motion—Jenkins raised the subject of the economy at a normal Tuesday morning Cabinet meeting. Wilson replied: 'We'll have a full discussion in about two or three weeks' time.' Jenkins retorted that this did not satisfy him, but Wilson prevented further discussion. However, on Thursday, 16 November, Wilson and Callaghan were ready to tell the Cabinet. As the meeting opened, the Prime Minister said: 'The Chancellor and I have an important statement to make. We must take it first and then deal with any other items for which there is time.' Then Callaghan spoke: 'I have decided that the pound must be devalued. If the Cabinet agrees, the necessary machinery will be set in motion and devaluation will be announced on Saturday. This is the unhappiest day of my life.'

During the last two days before 18 November, devaluation was widely expected, but the speculation derived from a false rumour on the BBC about Britain seeking a $1 billion loan, rather than through any leak of the Treasury's devaluation programme. At 9.30 p.m. on Saturday, 18 November the Treasury announced that the pound had been devalued from $2.80 to $2.40, and Wilson appeared on television to make his unfortunate remark about 'the pound in your pocket'.

Callaghan was now exhausted. In some respects his private attitudes—though not his public posture—had proved to be entirely correct; but he suffered the cumulative strain of executing over three years a policy which devaluation destroyed. On the evening of devaluation Callaghan wrote to Wilson resigning as Chancellor; he said that in finally advising devaluation to the Cabinet, 'I was very conscious that I was going back on pledges that I had given in good faith to a number of overseas countries about the value of their sterling holdings. No Chancellor of the Exchequer can escape this dilemma. But I do not think it right that I should continue in the office and so with the deepest regret I must ask you to accept my resignation.'

By taking full blame on himself in this way, Callaghan obscured the more complicated Cabinet relationships which had developed over sterling, especially since July 1966; above all, in his resignation letter he laid none of the blame on Wilson, the true architect of the anti-devaluation policy which had just crumbled. On the other hand, to have written more frankly about his own attitudes and Wilson's role since 1964 would have been not only politically unwise in terms of his own career, but probably fatal for the whole Government. Callaghan knew he had to present himself as the scapegoat, even if he felt he shouldered more of the blame than he deserved.

Callaghan's resignation was not announced immediately: he agreed to stay on at the Treasury to see the devaluation operation through Parliament. On Wednesday, 22 November he made a speech which many MPs regarded among his finest. After conceding that devaluation was 'a symbol that this country has slipped behind other nations', Callaghan gave a peroration quite out of keeping with his normal style: 'I want to see in this country a sense of self-discipline survive and grow which will enable us to combine the good things in life that the whole country wants. I want to see social democracy work and succeed, and I believe it can. But if it is to do so we have to look behind the economic motivation, and much deeper. We want a nation not only concerned with economic motivation, but a nation that is both proud and self-reliant, and compassionate.'

Despite his exhaustion, Callaghan showed in this speech that he had preserved his political skills intact. For while Wilson had

Callaghan's resignation letter—as yet unpublished—taking full blame for devaluation, Callaghan was using his week as 'caretaker' Chancellor to stake out his position for the future. The next morning's *Daily Telegraph* had no doubts what Callaghan meant. Under the headline 'Bid by Callaghan for Premiership', the paper's Political Correspondent H. B. Boyne wrote: '[Callaghan's speech] struck many MPs as a declaration that he holds himself available as a future leader of the Labour Party. To some it even sounded like an actual bid for the Premiership. A point on which practically everybody agreed was that Mr Callaghan was not signalling any intention to bow himself off the political scene . . . There was general agreement that Mr Callaghan's speech was on a much higher plane than the Prime Minister's a few hours earlier, and indeed than any other in the debate.'

A week later Wilson announced that Callaghan would switch jobs with Roy Jenkins, the Home Secretary. After a short holiday to recover from the traumas of devaluation, Callaghan began work in the quieter pastures of the Home Office.

Immediately after devaluation, verdicts on Callaghan's stewardship of the economy began to appear. An article by Peter Jay in *The Times* on 22 November provoked the strongest reaction. Jay had left the Treasury a few months earlier to become Economics Editor of *The Times*, where he scrupulously maintained his journalistic objectivity towards Callaghan, his father-in-law. But in his article following devaluation he made his opinion clear: the pound had been overvalued since 1962, and should have been devalued much earlier than it was. So who was to blame for the futile defence of the exchange rate? Jay concluded: 'Both Mr Macmillan and Mr Wilson were responsible: Mr Macmillan for presiding over the period in which the economic seed corn stemming from the 1949 devaluation was frittered away and the basic disequilibrium was generated; and Mr Wilson for refusing to admit the basic facts of the economic situation . . . But what of the role of the Chancellor? No one will perhaps ever know what in his heart Mr Callaghan's real attitude was, if indeed he had one. Like King Henry VIII's Cardinal Wolsey he judged that the only viable policy was the King's policy, whatever its strengths and weaknesses.'

The day the article appeared, Jay was scheduled to appear on a television panel of journalists to interview Wilson about devaluation. After reading what Jay had to say, Wilson vetoed Jay's television appearance; asked about the veto, Wilson said: 'I don't think it's right for me to comment on a very slanted article by a former civil servant because to put the record right on that particular article I would have to give a great deal of information that ought not to be made public, and in the national interest ought not and should not have been made public.' Wilson was referring to some of the information Jay had published to reach his conclusions—such as the Prime Minister's suppression of papers by economic advisers in 1965 and 1966 recommending devaluation. Commenting on Wilson's statement, Jay denied using any information he had gathered as a civil servant, or having spoken to Callaghan since well before devaluation.

The squabble over Jay's article and Wilson's television appearance heightened interest in the political battles surrounding devaluation. Meanwhile the more substantial point went undebated: was Jay's assessment of Wilson and Callaghan fair?

Jay was certainly correct in observing that Wilson, rather than Callaghan, led the battle for sterling. And his observation about Callaghan's 'real attitude'—'if indeed he had one ... He judged that the only viable policy was the King's policy'—was shrewd and well-informed. Whether this amounts to an adequate defence of Callaghan is another matter. We have seen that in October 1964 Callaghan fully accepted Wilson's save-the-pound economic strategy, arguing only, at one meeting, that the decision should not be taken so hastily. We have also seen that in July 1966 Callaghan told colleagues that devaluation would be necessary. Unlike George Brown, however, he made no serious attempt to change Cabinet policy: his advocacy of devaluation stemmed more from occasional bouts of acute frustration than from a coherent and sustained campaign to persuade other ministers that sterling was overvalued.

To this Callaghan can reply that opinion among his advisers was divided even as late as 1966: they did not become united in their opinions until the summer of 1967. But no Chancellor can escape the final responsibility for determining Treasury policy, even if it is then over-ruled by the Cabinet. Callaghan's decision, for three years, was not so much to have a pro-devaluation policy or an anti-devaluation policy, but to have *no* policy other than Wilson's—'the King's'.

If Jay's defence absolves Callaghan from taking all the blame for the Labour Government's mistakes over sterling, it suggests a different, though no less serious, criticism: that Callaghan was too weak a Chancellor to formulate and fight for policies he could believe in. Loyalty to a party, or a person, is highly creditable in a politician, and forms one of the consistent strands of Callaghan's career. But a loyalty which is devoid of any external reference to what is right or appropriate is a weakness which tends to cause trouble, as Callaghan's loyalty towards Wilson over sterling so savagely demonstrated.

A more fundamental criticism follows from this. In waging, and losing, the battle for sterling, the Government allowed Britain's economic structure to suffer serious damage. The 'scientific revolution' which Wilson had heralded in 1963 failed to materialise, and Callaghan's sequence of deflationary measures, starting in November 1964, ensured that the National Plan devised by his Cabinet rival George Brown would fail. Imperfect though it was, the plan provided a hope of reversing Britain's industrial decline; indeed, some left-wing Labour MPs who opposed the plan at the time (because it was launched by Brown, and Brown was too right-wing) now regret that they did not respond to it more positively.

This remains debated territory among economists; but there is considerable force in the argument advanced by Robert Bacon and Walter Eltis in *Britain's Economic Problem: Too Few Producers*: '[In 1966] Mr Brown and his advisers wanted to devalue . . . to provide an adequate balance of payments for the years ahead. This would have achieved the desired result of improving the balance of payments without prejudicing expansion if there had also been drastic cuts in consumption, so that extra resources could have gone to exports without damaging investment . . . Sadly, the Department of Economic Affairs failed to make out its case for the policies it wanted. There were severe expenditure cuts and no devaluation. Expansion therefore ceased, the National Plan was abandoned, and nothing was done to make it possible for the spare resources released to go to exports where they could lay a foundation for the future . . . In retrospect this was to prove the decisive turning-point after which the structure of the United Kingdom economy deteriorated almost without interruption.'

Callaghan's—and Wilson's—speeches from the time do not suggest that they grasped this point; neither do they supply any alternative economic theory to show how recovery and full employment could be achieved while defending sterling. Instead, holding the exchange rate became a question of honour—an end in itself—so that when devaluation did eventually occur, it automatically became a 'defeat', rather than a painful act of liberation. Callaghan may have been the prisoner of Wilson's decisions; and he may have been the victim of circumstances he was not equipped fully to comprehend. But he was the Chancellor, nonetheless.

It would be wrong to conclude an assessment of Callaghan's time at the Treasury without recording his one partial success and his one notable achievement. His partial success concerned tax reform. The corporation tax, capital gains tax and betting tax have all worked well and survived. The selective employment tax, however, did not last long: it was one of Kaldor's more ingenious ideas to boost employment in manufacturing industries, and penalise the service sector; but in operation it proved arguably too cumbersome and certainly too unpopular. The Conservatives finally abolished it in 1973 when the Heath Government introduced VAT. Callaghan's second tax failure was the wealth tax. He had first proposed such a tax in February 1963 when he was shadow Chancellor, and the idea proved popular throughout the Labour Party. But two months after taking office in October 1964 he surrendered to opposition from the Treasury and from foreign bankers: the idea had to wait until the next Labour Government ten years later to be revived. But against this disappointment, Callaghan can count the introduction of the regional employment premium in 1967 to his credit. The Conservatives described it as 'a nonsense', but in government carried on paying it.

While tax reform proved to be a partial success, Callaghan's actions to secure international monetary reform must count as an important achievement. In the mid-1960s the world's money system threatened to fall apart. For twenty years the arrangements hammered out at the Bretton Woods conference at the end of the Second World War had held together, and the International Monetary Fund and the World Bank became two of the most effective organisations within the United Nations. But by the mid-1960s America's dominance of the western world was being threatened by the revived economies of Europe and Japan, and the stresses among these countries—especially between the US and France—began to show at meetings of the IMF and the more select 'Group of Ten' (the Finance Ministers of the ten richest western countries).

The issue which caused most argument was at root simple, even if to the outsider somewhat abstruse: was world liquidity too great or too small, and what should be done about it? France maintained that too many dollars were circulating round world money markets, and that the system should be stabilised by restoring gold to the centre of international monetary arrangements. The United States argued that the real danger was too little liquidity, and that a new world paper money should be created, analogous to the paper money which circulates inside each country.

Callaghan served as chairman of the Group of Ten in 1966–7, the year when the dispute reached its climax. With considerable skill he secured agreement for a modest start to a paper-money experiment—Special Drawing Rights, which have since become an established and invaluable component of international government finance. Callaghan's friends say he is proud of this achievement; and with some justice.

It is an irony that Callaghan must savour more than anyone else that his most successful achievement as Chancellor was to preserve the ordered world of Bretton Woods—whereas twenty-three years earlier his opposition to it had been the cause of his career's only significant rebellion.

8

1967-70:
Home Secretary

'Our trimmer owneth a passion for liberty, yet so restricted that it doth not in the least impair or taint his allegiance.'
—THE MARQUIS OF HALIFAX, in *The Character of a Trimmer*

After two weeks' holiday to recover from the shell-shock of the Treasury, Callaghan took up his duties at the Home Office. His first act on re-entering the political mainstream was very nearly a disaster.

On 11 December 1967, at St Stephen's Tavern in Westminster, he made his first off-the-record political speech for years when he addressed the dinner of the 'Under 40 Group'—around sixty younger Labour MPs who had entered Parliament in 1964 or 1966. In the course of his remarks he suggested that Labour's hallowed policy of banning the supply of arms to South Africa might have to be revised or even abandoned. Horrified MPs from all wings of the party tabled a motion reaffirming the commitment to a total arms embargo and a blazing argument broke out across the PLP. The motion was signed by 136 Labour MPs: this seems to have convinced Wilson to oppose Healey and Brown, both of whom wanted to re-negotiate contracts with Pretoria. At a Cabinet meeting on 15 December, Callaghan complained bitterly that within ten minutes of a private speech the protesters were lobbying the Chief Whip, and that this was unfair. Barbara Castle asked acidly whether, if the Home Secretary took that tone, he would mind if she also spoke 'off the record' on her disagreements with the Cabinet's Vietnam policy. Callaghan, by now in an uncomfortable position, said that she would be popular if she said that, but 'I was trying to educate them in the need for unpopular policies'. The dust soon settled, and the embargo was upheld. But

Callaghan was left with a large number of potential enemies.

He did little enough to re-inspire confidence when, speaking in the House of Commons on 20 February 1968, he suddenly announced in an exchange on violent crime that 'the police are having considerable success in these matters at the moment. Less than three hours ago one of those responsible for the murder at Fulham was arrested at Bolton in Lancashire.' Despite the uproar which followed this gaffe pre-judging the verdict of the courts, he went on to say 'the man who committed murder in Acton this morning has also been arrested'. The hubbub then reached a pitch where his junior minister Dick Taverne had to slide along the bench and caution him to say that the men in question were only 'alleged' to have committed crimes.

As the *Daily Telegraph* political correspondent wrote the next day: 'Reporters in the Press Gallery heard Mr Callaghan's words with a sinking heart. Many of them have been trained from their earliest days in magistrates' courts to use "helping the police with their inquiries", but on no account to ascribe responsibility.' Lamely Callaghan concluded, 'I want to bring the attention of the House to one thing only, that the police, in so far as they are responsible, are acting in as good a way as they can.' There were scattered demands in the press and in Parliament for Callaghan to resign, but it was generally agreed that only a slip—albeit a dangerous slip—had been made.

After the incident, Harold Wilson remarked to a colleague that 'Jim isn't as much a Minister of Justice as a Minister of Police.' There is some truth in the aside: Callaghan had been the first paid Parliamentary adviser to the Police Federation, and had won tremendous popularity among policemen for his skilful lobbying of the '£1,000 a year bobby' campaign when R. A. Butler was Home Secretary. In 1959, with Labour fortunes at a low ebb, and his own Cardiff South-East majority down to a precarious 868, Callaghan even discussed leaving Parliament to take up a full-time job with the Police Federation. The talks did not lead anywhere, but Callaghan's relations with the police remained extremely close and only suffered late in his tenure at the Home Office when general expenditure cuts were made and the police force had to bear its share of the burden.

The one serious exception to this harmony concerned the 1968 Race Relations Bill, which Callaghan inherited from his predecessor, Roy Jenkins. This made a wide range of forms of racial discrimination a criminal offence. The Police Federation disliked the Bill; they disliked even more a new clause in the Police (Discipline) Code which made it an offence for the police themselves to discriminate against coloured citizens. When Callaghan visited the Federation's 1968 conference, the chairman, Reginald Webb, received a thunderous ovation when he said: 'There is not a man or woman in this room who does not feel sickened that such a clause was judged to be necessary. It is a gross insult even to suggest it.' Callaghan replied: 'I agree that this [clause] will affect neither your attitude to the coloured communities nor your responsibility ... It will neither subtract from nor add to your duty—but it must be spelt out.'

Apart from this one issue, there was, as Federation men used to say, nothing of the wet liberal about the new Home Secretary. Where Jenkins had studied each topic, and each brief, with painstaking care, Callaghan—with memories of the avalanche of Treasury paperwork agonisingly fresh in his mind—would dispose as swiftly as possible with the red boxes of documents which his officials laid before him. His very first red box occupied him for just forty-five minutes, causing one stunned official to remark: 'Home Secretary, you have just done three weeks' work.'

But there was a more fundamental difference between Callaghan and Jenkins. Jenkins had made his name by sponsoring and supporting all manner of reformist, and often controversial, measures, relating to capital punishment, homosexuality and abortion. Interviewed in the *Sunday Times* in January 1968, Callaghan displayed little of Jenkins's libertarian passions. Would he be a radical reformist? asked Hugo Young. 'I would see myself as a reforming realist.' 'What about the "radical"?' 'That is included in the "reform". If you like, I shall be a radical reforming realist. Any combination you like ... I have prejudices. I suppose Home Secretaries are allowed them.'

Young pointed out that during his term as Chancellor, Callaghan had had a poor voting record; he had not, for example, turned up to vote in the crucial division on capital punishment in 1965. Callaghan replied that he looked on these debates, 'with respect, as opportunities for getting on with other things'. He described Lord Cobbold, the Lord Chamberlain, who had become famous for his restrictive censorship judgements, as 'urbane and civilised'. He opposed capital punishment even though he had not voted. As for the other reforms: 'Abortion, yes as it finally came out; homosexuality I was indifferent to.' He referred several times to the vital role of his 'God-given common sense' and remarked 'Of course, I cannot bear the young men with hair hanging over their shoulders.' Asked whether he felt the search powers contained in the Dangerous Drugs Act were too severe he said confidently: 'I have known the police for many years and I doubt whether they will abuse their power in that direction.' In short, the new Home Secretary held very conventional views; and he was not prepared to take any risks by running ahead of public opinion in the way Jenkins had. Dick Taverne, who served under Callaghan at the Home Office for some months, recalls that 'his strength lay in handling people rather than issues, and he felt that politicians should reflect popular views more than try to lead them'.

Passports and Prejudice: the Immigration Act of 1968

'Probably the most shameful measure that Labour members have ever been asked by their whips to support.' Thus wrote *The Times* in the last week of February 1968, in an editorial attack upon the Commonwealth Immigrants Act which was rushed through Parliament in three panicky days that month with 35 Labour MPs voting against it. With the passing of that Act, British law for the first time took note of racial differences between its citizens and subjects, and coldly calibrated their varying rights to enter the country. Seen in retrospect (and also to some extent, remarked at the time) late February 1968 was the point at which large numbers of the liberal intelligentsia withdrew their active support from what Hugh Gaitskell had called 'the party of conscience and reform'. It was, taken together with the Tet offensive in Vietnam and the public spending cuts announced by Roy Jenkins, a springtime of disillusion for Labour's rank and file.

Callaghan, however, clearly thought that in this matter he was heeding the wishes of public opinion, even when filtered to him by Duncan Sandys, Enoch Powell and the other campaigners against the right of Kenyan Asians with British passports to settle here. In this, he was probably right. But the actual process of the Bill's birth and gestation did not make him any more popular.

During and after the independence which Britain conceded to her East African colonies in the early sixties, a bargain was struck which enabled Asian citizens to opt either for British citizenship or citizenship of the country in which they lived. Iain Macleod, who was Colonial Secretary at the time, wrote during the 1968 controversy that this committed Britain to allowing them to enter the country 'under certain circumstances which have now arisen. We did it. We meant to do it. And in any event we had no other choice', he said. Five other junior ministers of the same period agreed with him—Britain was legally and morally bound to her Asian citizens, just as France had been over the question of French Algeria after the Evian treaty which gave Algeria sovereignty.

Later in 1968, Callaghan was to describe the Asians in an unhappy phrase as 'lemming-like'. His first serious mistake in February's controversy was to exaggerate and confuse the vexed question of numbers. Nobody, it turned out, had any idea of the real numbers of Asians entitled to come to Britain. The Kenya Government was proceeding with an 'Africanisation by stages' policy, and it was not until various politicians on the right, most notably Duncan Sandys, had prophesied the arrival of 250,000 people that any real exodus from Kenya started. It began precisely *because* many Kenyan Asians feared legislation in London which would slam the door. Richard Kershaw wrote from Nairobi at the time that 'there is absolutely no doubt that the noises from London about the possibility of new limitations on entry were the primary cause of the panic. To use a ghastly metaphor, it was not so much a matter of leaving a sinking ship, as trying to board one that was about to leave the shore.' Numbers, then, were to some extent a self-inflicted problem for Callaghan. The drafting and arguing of the Bill were the next problems.

He claimed at the time that the Government had had contingency legislation ready for some time. This was not true. Roy Jenkins had, in fact, discussed and then rejected the need for such a plan when he was at the Home Office. In Cabinet on 22 February, Callaghan argued successfully for legislation against the stiff opposition of the Commonwealth Secretary George

Thomson. The argument against Callaghan, inside and outside the Government, was roughly along the lines of Lord Jowitt in the case of Joyce *v.* the Director of Public Prosecutions: 'To me, my Lords, it appears that the Crown in issuing a passport is assuming an onerous burden, and the holder of the passport is acquiring substantial privileges. Armed with that document the holder may demand ... that he be treated as a British subject.' Callaghan intended overturning this principle. It was not a decision to be rushed or equivocated; and he secured a terrible press for himself by not staying on top of his brief.

At 8 p.m. the next day, 23 February, Callaghan told the House that 'I was asked what I would do about a man who was thrown out of work and ejected from the country. We shall have to take him. We cannot do anything else in those circumstances.' Yet later that night, the Solicitor-General, Sir Arthur Irvine, said that 'mass expulsions would swamp the whole procedure provided for in the Bill. All one can say is that in that kind of situation one would apply measures that seemed appropriate.' At tea-time the next day, Callaghan tried but failed to extricate himself by saying 'If there is said to be a difference in tone between what two Ministers say, that is something for people to assess. The Home Office have been besieged with inquiries all week.' It did not have the ring of confidence about it. In his main speech on the Bill, Callaghan said at one point that he had neither the funds nor the staff to set up any appeals procedure. Under pressure a short time later on in the same speech, he agreed to set up a tribunal of two people and said they would have to be enough. But, as one Cabinet colleague pointed out afterwards, a few minutes earlier he had not had the people or the money even for that. 'It sounded', the minister said, 'as if Jim was making it up as he went along.'

The appeals procedure, in fact, was a large part of his undoing. In Cabinet on 22 February he had turned down suggestions for a 'concession' on quotas, and for another 'concession' on appeals machinery. The January cuts in public expenditure, he said, made it too expensive. But eventually he had to climb down because of back-bench pressure in the first instance, and also because three Kenyan Asians took Britain to the European Commission on Human Rights and successfully demonstrated discrimination. The result of this was the Immigration Appeals Act of 1969, which repaired some of the damage done to race relations and civil liberties in the interim, but did not alter the basic and disturbing fact that 'patriality' had become a legal criterion in Britain, with grandfathers or fathers having to be born here (motherhood did not cut any ice) if equal rights were to be claimed. Callaghan had created a group of people, formerly under British protection, who had a nationality but no homeland.

'Callamandering': the Boundary Commission dispute

In the summer of 1969, it fell to Callaghan to face unprecedented Conservative fury over the re-drawing of parliamentary boundaries. There were at the time 47 constituencies with more than 80,000 electors, and the last revision of boundaries in 1954 had attempted to guard against this. By convention, Boundary Commission reports are implemented fairly swiftly and without demur. The problem this time was that the Tories believed they could gain from between 10 to 15 seats by the redistribution, and most political analysts tended to bear this out. In essence the Boundaries Commission report proposed raising the number of constituencies from 630 to 635; it would divide up the most heavily populated seats, most of which covered new towns or dormitory towns outside the large cities; this on balance would increase the strength of the Conservatives. At the same time, the Commission suggested merging a number of the smaller city-centre seats which had lost people owing to rehousing; this would harm Labour.

As an exercise in objective calculation, the Boundaries Commission's work could not be faulted. But its consequences were depressing for Labour; and the party still recalled how it had been 'cheated' of the 1951 General Election, when Labour won the most votes, but the Conservatives won the most seats. Even so, any parliamentary democracy depends heavily on acceptance of an agreed set of rules. Callaghan came very close to uprooting this important tradition.

In June 1969 Callaghan told the Commons after the appearance of the report that instead of raising the number of MPs to 635, the Government proposed to reduce the figure from 630 to 626. In addition, he made it clear that there would be no general revision of boundaries before the next election. He announced that the date—9 November—stipulated as the target date for the changes would be altered by legislation. 'There is no magic about this date', he said; 'it is not divinely ordained, and what Parliament has done, Parliament can undo.' By this time, the Opposition were in uproar, and the phrase 'Callamandering' began to be heard freely in the lobbies. Their rage knew no bounds when the Home Secretary announced that there would be no delay in the implementation of the commission's recommendations for London (where Labour was expected to benefit from the changes).

The ostensible reason for this manœuvre was that the Redcliffe-Maud report on local government had not yet been published, and that it was desirable for the two sets of political boundaries to match one another as nearly as possible. This did not save Callaghan from a very embarrassing series of debates and exchanges in the House. Eventually, the Lords prevented him from implementing the report as far as London went, but the Labour majority in the Commons was enough to ensure that the 1970 election was fought on the same boundaries as the election of 1966. It was not an edifying episode, though technically Callaghan was right in maintaining that Parliament was the master of the timing and procedure.

In one little-noticed exchange, with Sir David Renton, a Conservative spokesman, Callaghan even showed himself unaware of the boundaries of his own Cardiff constituency (see p. 126).

The boundaries dispute has an ironic postscript. The 1970 Heath Government did alter the boundaries, and it was widely expected that the Conservatives would benefit at the following General Election. In the event, the opposite happened: in February 1974 the Conservatives won more votes than Labour, but Labour won more seats. It was the 1951 General Election in reverse.

Civil Liberty

Throughout his tenure at the Home Office, Callaghan found it easier to deal with cases than with principles. On one occasion shortly after taking office, there were reports in the press that the headmaster of a Catholic approved school in the Isle of Wight had struck one of his charges, knocking him to the ground. Coming as it did so soon after the Court Lees inquiry into brutality in approved schools (where Jenkins had distinguished himself) the case engaged Callaghan's full attention. Dick Taverne was asked to report and recommend. He reported that the headmaster was a quick-tempered but kind and devoted man, and that the school was in any case a denominational one and outside Home Office jurisdiction. Callaghan, however, incensed at the thought of violence to children, asked to see the governors of the school and persuaded them to sack the headmaster.

In this particular case, involving a borderline judgement, Callaghan took the 'liberal' side. On issues involving wider principles, he was somewhat less courageous. Having turned down the recommendations of the Wootton Committee on the use of cannabis (they wanted it legalised under certain conditions), he told the Police Federation: 'I am not ready to take the risks of permissiveness.' The remark can be taken as a motif for his entire policy at the Home Office: on mandatory sentences for violent crime, he had a public dispute with Lord Parker of Waddington, then Lord Chief Justice; on demands for independent inquiries into allegations against the police, his movement was so slow as to be imperceptible; on the powers of the Ombudsman, he argued in Cabinet that ministers should be able to overrule specific decisions; on liaising with academic criminologists, he astounded an expert meeting at Cambridge by announcing that he would simply read out a departmental brief—instead of discussing and defending his own attitudes.

The Fabian conference in October 1968 was equally dismayed to hear Callaghan reject conjugal visits for long-term prisoners by arguing 'The sophistication of crime nowadays, and the growing organisation of crime, does mean that even wives can be a great source of ... I will not go into details ... you must let your imagination work.'

He also proceeded cautiously on the subject of public order. In 1968 and 1969 a number of angry political demonstrations, usually involving students and young people, took place on the issues of Vietnam and South Africa. Here, Callaghan's instincts for public opinion and his close and warm relationship with the police served him well. Writing of the massive march through London against the American war in Vietnam, which was scheduled for 27 October 1968 he describes how 'Quintin Hogg came to see me at the Home Office and, his composure deserting him, proposed that I should confine the Guards to their London barracks so that they could be available to put down any revolt. He further suggested that I should close all the main line railway stations and have every car and coach coming into London searched.' The mood of authoritarian hysteria in the House of Commons was even greater, with strident Tory attacks on 'foreign scum' and 'red revolution'. On all sides, Callaghan was urged to ban the demonstration. But, advised by the police that such things are harder to ban than they are to control, he stood firm and 'the day ended with the remnants of the marchers and the police singing "Auld Lang Syne" as they broke off the engagement'. There could be no more perfect example of Callaghan's skill at man-management—he himself made a personal appearance in the disputed territory of Grosvenor Square, and set the seal on a day's work well done.

The 1970 Cricket Tour by the South African side presented a thornier problem. For one thing, there is a difference between a one-off demonstration and a series of Test Matches with a likely succession of confrontations between anti-apartheid protesters and the police. For another, the Conservative Party had already begun to make 'law and order' a serious election issue. Debating the no less controversial rugby tour of the previous autumn, Callaghan had told the House on 17 November 1969: 'I do not believe it would be right for the Government to step into this matter and to try to ensure that the tour is not played.'

But in February 1970 he approached the MCC to tell them that the cost to them of providing police protection could be as much as a quarter of a million pounds. He did so in order to forestall a move, made at that month's meeting of the Labour National Executive Committee, to have the tour cancelled by government intervention. In March, during a meeting of ministers at Chequers, he opposed the use of police on a wide scale against demonstrators, and cited recent disturbances at Nanterre University in Paris as a warning against 'tough measures'. He also revealed that he was examining the law of trespass (which the Tories had announced they would strengthen), but did not hope for very much from it.

Meanwhile, advance intelligence on disruptive activities was becoming clearer every day. Imaginative anti-apartheid campaigners had plans to buy blocks of tickets for the offending matches. They had mirrors to shine in the players' eyes, and wickets all over the country ran the risk of being dug up. However there were two other, more practical, considerations that finally prompted Callaghan to take action. The first was that the first Test Match was scheduled to begin on 18 June—one of the most likely dates for a General Election (and, indeed, the one finally chosen). It could fatally wound Labour's prospects for the Government to seem unable to maintain law and order on the very day voters went to the polls.

The second consideration was no less serious. As mid-May approached, numbers of Commonwealth countries announced their withdrawal from that year's Commonwealth Games. On the day that Kenya and Zambia did so, Callaghan announced that he would see the Cricket Council and ask them to call off the tour officially. The Police Federation delegates, who were meeting for their annual conference, cheered loudly when they heard the news that they would be spared 'a long hot summer'. Confirmation was not long in coming—the Cricket Council accepted Callaghan's 'stick and carrot' offer. The stick was the threat of wrecking the Commonwealth Games, which he pointed out would be laid at their door. The carrot was the acceptance by the Government of responsibility for the cancellation, which would enable the Cricket Council to show an alibi if necessary. Honour and face were saved all round, and although some Tories fumed at 'surrender to anarchy', they could not deny the consummate skill and tact of the Home Secretary.

Callaghan's term at the Home Office was most sharply illuminated by public relations triumphs of that kind—notably in Ulster (see Chapter 10). But reflecting on the wide range of his work, he himself emphasised other things. In a *Guardian* interview on 29 May 1970—at the height of the General Election campaign—Callaghan said:

If you ask me what I want to spend my time on—and what I

have to some extent achieved—it would be the beginnings of the long reform of the prisons to ensure rehabilitation as well as proper control; the Children and Young Persons Act; and the urban programme and community development.

So far as prisons are concerned, buildings are involved and this will take a long time to achieve—this and the recruitment of staff are obviously long-term issues and I have got a bigger building programme in new prisons than we have had in this century. The Children and Young Persons Act has set a new series of standards both for care and control of young persons. These two things, care and control, are different sides of the same thing. For instance, I am very interested in these as yet undeveloped notions of weekend, semi-custodial treatment, for example by camps, where young people are told by a court: 'This is the kind of work we expect you to do for the next X months at weekends.' It is that field of care in which I feel we have got a lot of opportunities.

Today many of the 1960s assumptions about social policy are being questioned; but whether or not Callaghan's particular initiatives prove in the long run to have been sensible, there can be no doubt that this was the aspect of Home Office work with which Callaghan felt most at ease.

Having started as an unhappy and defeated ex-Chancellor, Callaghan finished his stewardship of the Home Office as a confident and restored man. He believed that his espousal of 'safe' reforms and rejection of more daring ones had matched the public mood. As he once said—and in saying, wrote the motto for his Home Secretaryship—'I suppose what worries me about the libertarians is that they may lose our supporters—the people in the Cardiff back streets who I know and feel at home with.'

In April 1970 he felt sufficiently confident that Labour would not lose its supporters to tell Wilson that it did not matter which date the Prime Minister chose for the General Election: Labour would win with ease in either June or October. For once Callaghan had misjudged the electorate. On 18 June they voted Conservative (or abstained from voting Labour) in sufficient numbers to lose Labour the election. But whatever their reason for doing so, it cannot have been any excess of libertarian zeal on Callaghan's part.

9

1967-70: The Road Back

'The relationship between trade unions and government is exceedingly complex.'

—TUC evidence to the Donovan Commission on the Reform of Trade Unions and Employers' Associations

Callaghan's work as Home Secretary between 1967 and 1970 did not command his undivided attention. During a Cabinet meeting on 11 January 1968, he passed a brief note to Barbara Castle saying he would like to have a general chat: he felt the two of them were drifting apart, and now that he had more spare time he would like to try to rebuild their friendship. Callaghan soon changed his mind.

The careful choice of his friends and enemies has always been a characteristic of Callaghan's career. In opposition between 1951 and 1964, as we have seen, he built up his party following by judiciously picking the right sides in the right battles—rather than by establishing a coherent political philosophy and fighting for its acceptance. From 1964 to 1967, however, Callaghan had little chance to continue his rise in the Labour Party by his traditional route; instead he had to rely on his performance in office as Chancellor of the Exchequer—a far more precarious basis for consolidating popularity than his manœuvring in opposition had been.

In the early months of the Labour Government Callaghan had succeeded in retaining his place on the National Executive Committee with some ease. In December 1964 he came fifth in the constituency section, out of seven successful candidates: local parties gave him 524,000 votes. In September 1965 his vote rose to 542,000, and he climbed to fourth place. But by October 1966, the succession of economic crises and deflationary measures was beginning to harm Callaghan's standing; he lost almost 20 per cent of his support, falling back to fifth place with 447,000 votes. Callaghan feared losing his place altogether in 1967. And this would have deprived him of his one independent source of party influence—at exactly the time when his ministerial fortunes were in such low water.

But then with one bound, he was free. In 1967 the party's treasurership fell vacant, when Dai Davies left to run the British Iron and Steel Confederation. Labour's treasurer is elected by *all* party members—which means in practice that it is in the gift of the large trade unions, whose block votes swamp those of the constituency parties. Callaghan stood against Foot, and obtained the support of most unions: the one major exception was the Transport and General Workers' Union. Callaghan defeated Foot by 4,312,000 votes to 2,025,000.

From then on, Callaghan's place on the NEC was never at risk. He defeated Foot again in 1968 (by 4,039,000 to 1,449,000) and 1969 (by 4,429,000 to 1,621,000). His party power base had shifted to more secure ground; and with his appointment as Home Secretary at the end of 1967, Callaghan had—as he wrote in his note—more free time. His friend-making could resume in earnest, as could the consolidation of his power base in the party.

Callaghan's tactics were to cost him a certain amount of his Cabinet colleagues' respect, but he seems to have calculated that as being at a low ebb anyway. On 28 May 1968, speaking to the conference of the Fire Brigades' Union, Callaghan said that the penal clauses of the Prices and Incomes Bill, then before Parliament, would have to be reconsidered at the end of 1969. By that time, he announced, 'when the current powers expire, we shall have had legislation concerned with wages for three and a half years. That is long enough. At the end of that time we shall still need an incomes policy—I believe strongly in that—but it must be based on voluntary methods and not on legislation.'

Barbara Castle, who had been appointed Employment Secretary just seven weeks earlier, was appalled at his cynicism—for the original wage controls had been introduced in 1966 when Callaghan himself was Chancellor. She suspected him of currying favour with the trade unions for the purpose of consolidating his party treasurership.

Castle had two further reasons for her fury. For one thing,

instead of notifying her about his speech—as etiquette among ministers demanded—Callaghan merely sent a copy of it to the Department of Employment and Productivity on the day it was made. A 'compliments' slip attached to the speech did not entitle it to the most prompt attention: by the time it was read it had appeared on news agency tapes. And finally, Castle was annoyed because as recently as March Callaghan had argued for the reactivation of part 2 of the 1966 Act, as reinforced by part 2 of the 1967 Act, which provided for statutory warning and notification of wage proposals or settlements. Wherever his sudden opposition to statute came from, it self-evidently was not from principle.

At a Cabinet meeting on 30 May, Wilson attacked Callaghan for pre-empting government policy and for making life difficult for the ministers concerned with enforcing it. Callaghan, though, was unrepentant, and replied confidently: 'we all know we can't legislate again in 1969, don't we?'—a remark well calculated to sow disquiet. A few days later, Wilson publicly repudiated Callaghan's views at the TUC. But the Home Secretary's withers were unwrung. He had decided where his road back lay: it lay through the trade unions. Whatever the price in unpopularity behind the doors of the Cabinet room, he was prepared to pay it.

The next test came fairly swiftly. Throughout the late spring and early summer of 1968 there had been rumours about who would succeed Len Williams as General Secretary of the Labour Party. Wilson and his closest associates were keen that the job should go to Anthony Greenwood—a friend of Wilson's for some years, a man with an undistinguished ministerial record but a radical reputation and some standing in the constituencies. George Brown, who according to Wilson's memoirs had promised to back whomever Wilson nominated, agreed that Greenwood would be best if Alf Allen, the leader of the Shopworkers' Union, could not be induced to stand. He could not, and Greenwood's name went forward to the Committee of Selection, who agreed to nominate him to the NEC in the absence of Allen. But at its meeting on 26 June, the Committee of Selection also suggested another name for consideration: Harry Nicholas, a veteran TGWU figure and an ex-Treasurer of the party.

Two names, then, went forward to the National Executive on 24 July. The miners' leader Joe Gormley moved the acceptance of the sub-committee report recommending Greenwood; then, without warning, Brown proposed Nicholas. Faced with the choice, the trade union vote went for Nicholas, slowly followed by the women's vote (which largely depends on trade-union block votes for the NEC); then up went the hand of the trade unions' new ally—Jim Callaghan. By 14 votes to 12 the NEC chose Nicholas. Greenwood was disappointed—but Wilson was livid.

There have been persistent stories which do not seem to bear examination, of sick men brought from their beds to vote on this occasion. But there was certainly a great deal of lobbying, and nobody doubted the part played by Callaghan. The following morning, the Parliamentary Labour Party was astonished to hear him launch an appeal at its general meeting for loyalty and unity, going on to flay the Tory press for trying to crucify the Prime Minister. Wilson, who was sitting on the podium with him, did not join in the very muted reception which Callaghan's speech finally received. For Castle, it was another of the occasions which confirmed her rapidly growing view that trade-union conservatism and self-interest were the greatest threats both to the country and the party.

Throughout this period, Callaghan was well aware that his image in the country needed refurbishing, and that although he might be building a solid base with the trade unions he was not a popular Home Secretary with Labour MPs. As with his views on incomes policy, this caused trouble for him in the Cabinet. For example, he displayed great anxiety over the Seebohm Report on local authority personal social services, not for any provision made therein but because he feared that the Home Office would lose some of its power by having to relinquish its child care responsibilities.

In mid-July, he tried to insist on making the announcement to the House about the Seebohm Report, and Wilson told Crossman in an aside that Callaghan was 'fighting for his life'. In the end Wilson made the Commons statement himself, confirming that some powers would be transferred, arguably because he felt Callaghan had been getting away with too much. One of the staff then at Number Ten remembers Wilson saying at this time:

'Whenever Jim tries to be a Young Turk I always know about it before he does.'

After the bruising experience of Chancellorship and the sometimes clumsy effect he created at the Home Office ('From Labour's Selwyn Lloyd to Labour's Henry Brooke' commented Peter Jenkins of the *Guardian*) Callaghan may not have looked at this time a very formidable opponent or tactician. But the next battle was to be fought on ground which favoured the genial power broker, and fought in terms which he understood best. 'The soul of the Labour movement' was about to be auctioned.

Labour's programme for growth, redistribution and investment had been torpedoed long before Barbara Castle arrived in St James's Square to shoulder the task of Employment, Productivity and, as it turned out, union reform. The Government had downgraded the Department of Economic Affairs, and lost the great trade union 'Mr Fixit' Ray Gunter, who had departed, in one of his only two memorable phrases, to 'the folk from which he came'.

Elements of those 'folk', Wilson now firmly believed, were the root cause of Labour's economic failure and of the party's unpopularity with floating voters. In his opinion, the trade unions' links with the party—symbolised by Transport House, headquarters of the Transport Workers' Union, as well as of the Labour Party—were working only one way. The seamen's strike of 1966, which he blamed for 'blowing the Government off course', had only been ended after weeks of paralysis at the ports and an allegation by Wilson, widely derided in the majority of newspapers, that the strike leaders of one of the most staid unions in the country were under the controlling influence of the Communist Party. Again, in November 1967 Wilson had had to contend with a bitter and damaging dispute at the Liverpool docks, which he always believed had contributed to devaluation and the general collapse of international confidence.

In 1965 Gunter, then Minister of Labour, had appointed a Royal Commission, headed by Lord Donovan, on trade union reform. Its findings were published in June 1968, soon after Barbara Castle arrived at the newly named Department of Employment. Its publication posed an awkward tactical, as well as policy, problem for the Government: the Conservative Party, with its document *Fair Deal at Work*, published in April 1968, had already anticipated Donovan's conclusions with some accuracy; and the party clearly signalled its determination to fight the next General Election on a platform of bringing trade unions under more rigid legal constraints than ever before. The Cabinet knew, and Wilson knew in particular, that this would be a very tough strategy to oppose.

Moreover, at the time it seemed clear from incidents such as an unofficial inter-union dispute at the Girling brake factory in Cheshire in the autumn of 1968 that the basic diagnosis of the Donovan Commission was correct—in Britain there were two tiers to industrial relations. The old carthorse of trade union authority apparently lumbered on, and after honour had been satisfied by a few days lost in a strike, an executive committee could usually be conciliated by the Ministry's patient officials or else offered tea and sandwiches at the eleventh hour in Downing Street. But increasingly, the shop stewards and rank-and-file militants were able to enforce wage drift on national settlements by short, sharp, localised strikes. The image of the wildcat became a stock one in the newspapers, and the Government found it both economically irritating and politically damaging. (Management responsibility for industrial unrest did not figure strongly in media coverage or government debate, excepting occasional platitudes about 'both sides of industry'.)

Although they were keen to devise a new, tougher policy towards the unions, Wilson and Castle knew there were obstacles lying in the way of its success. Ever since Callaghan's speech to the Fire Brigades' Union in May 1968, they had known that he was a potential enemy, and he gave them further proof of his attitude that autumn at the pre-party-conference NEC meeting, where he urged Castle to give the Labour movement an undertaking that the penal incomes policy powers would be scrapped on the expiry of the existing policy the following year.

The NEC defeated Callaghan but only on the casting vote of the chairman, Eirene White. Wilson and Castle thought him unreliable as well as disloyal, and felt that he might disgorge to his union friends the plans for trade-union reform that they were making, if he got premature notice of them. Wilson and Castle, therefore, did not consult or inform Callaghan, and concentrated instead on cementing the loyalty of Roy Jenkins, which proved much easier. They thereby ensured Callaghan's unremitting opposition to the proposals when they were published.

In early January 1969, Castle laid the new policy before the Cabinet. It took the form of a White Paper, to be called *In Place of Strife*, a title which evoked that of a book by Aneurin Bevan (*In Place of Fear*): a neat piece of psychological warfare thought up by Barbara Castle's husband Ted. It aimed to cut away the ground beneath Tory propaganda, but also to restore order in industry. It contained three proposals which, by any standard, were bound to be controversial. The first was the power it gave to a minister to order twenty-eight days of 'conciliation pause', during which work would be resumed pending negotiation. In the meantime, the *status quo ante* would apply; for example, a worker who had been dismissed would keep his or her job for the time being. Second, the minister was to have power to impose solutions on inter-union or demarcation disputes which had so far defeated the TUC or the Commission on Industrial Relations. Third, the White Paper proposed giving the minister powers to order a strike ballot in certain circumstances. This stipulation, which was a particular favourite of Wilson's, was made in order to avert such incidents as the threatened engineering strike in the autumn of 1968, where it was felt that Hugh Scanlon was more militant than his members and that the strike, had it been called, would have been catastrophic in its results. The Government planned to enforce the legislation by fines, to be levied by industrial courts, rather than traditional courts of law.

Callaghan, predictably, was against these proposals, and for particular, as well as general, reasons. As party Treasurer he inquired how Wilson and Castle thought they could raise an election war-chest from the trade unions if they carried on in this way. Other ministers, for a wide variety of reasons, were either sceptical or hostile; the notable opponents were Richard Crossman, Richard Marsh, Judith Hart and Anthony Crosland. Roy Mason also took a hand in criticism, and the upshot was that six meetings of the Cabinet were required to secure Cabinet approval. A less determined woman than Castle might have seen the writing on the wall at that point. The Labour correspondent of *The Times* argued that she was proposing 'enough government intervention to risk antagonising the trade unions but not enough to have any major impact on the country's main industrial problem'; and he was not to be lightly set aside since he (Eric Wigham) had himself been a member of the Donovan Commission.

A furious and crippling strike at Fords in February 1969 nevertheless confirmed both Castle and the Prime Minister on their chosen course. Fords had recourse to the courts, the workers ignored the proceedings, and public opinion, never very sympathetic towards car-workers, grew more heated. Wilson made a fighting speech in which he said: 'I want it to be clearly understood that the Government means business about these proposals. All that has happened in the last three weeks provides powerful support for the measures we shall be introducing in Parliament.' His speech struck the very note which had been putting Callaghan's teeth on edge—and the teeth of many union leaders and trade union MPs. Was it right for a Labour Prime Minister to talk about the unions as if they were the root cause of the nation's difficulties? Gut reactions began to be felt throughout the Labour movement, and who better to respond to them than the man with the unrivalled capacity for summing up traditional and fraternal emotions in the party?

Callaghan was not slow to seize his chance. On 26 March 1969 the Labour Party National Executive Committee met to discuss the proposals. A motion had already been circulated to members, and was proposed by Joe Gormley; it committed those present 'to inform the Minister that they cannot agree to support any legislation being introduced based on all the suggestions contained in that document'. 'All' really meant the ballots and the cooling-off periods. Contrary to the press reports of the time, which had Barbara Castle amending only a second minor sentence of the motion, she proposed an amendment which deleted Gormley's main point and substituted 'welcomes the Minister's assurance that there will be the fullest consultation with the trade unions before legislation is framed'. This amendment was defeated by fifteen votes to seven. Gormley's original motion was then carried by sixteen votes to five. (It was observed by some ministerial delegates present that by design or mistake, Callaghan voted for both motions.)

Tom Driberg recalls watching the hands go up round the table against Barbara Castle, seeing Callaghan watching the hands, and seeing him cast his vote with the expected majority on Gormley's motion. It was a constitutionally shattering situation, and with the Prime Minister away in an effort to mediate in the bloody Nigerian civil war, there was a period of suspended animation. To all intents and purposes, Callaghan might just as well have publicised his opposition to government policy on television or in Parliament. NEC meetings are not famous for their confidentiality, and this one was to become headline news very quickly. It soon emerged that Callaghan had not just registered a vote against the package, but had actually spoken out against the penal clauses which were the heart of the matter. This was rank opposition rather than mere dissent.

It did not take very long for the reverberations of Callaghan's action to find their way around the party and back to him. Speaking in his own constituency of Grimsby, Anthony Crosland said that 'if some of our comrades, high or low, do not like what the Government proposes, let them argue as hard as they like until the decision is taken. But once it is taken, let them stop'. He went on to recall the advice given by Clement Attlee to Harold Laski— 'A period of silence on your part would be welcome.' There was no veiling the attack on Callaghan, though whether or not Crosland knew of the old friendship between Callaghan and Laski is uncertain. Transport House made life even more difficult for the Government by excising this passage from the circulated version of the speech and, as usual, deceiving nobody.

On 3 April, Wilson returned from Nigeria and called a Cabinet meeting. He reminded ministers that *In Place of Strife* was a statement of policy and not a discussion document—though he did not single out any particular minister for criticism—and left for a holiday in the Scilly Isles shortly afterwards. The party's General Secretary Harry Nicholas, however, was making speech after speech saying the exact opposite; that the White Paper was still under discussion, that there were all sorts of loose ends to be tied up, and that any minister or indeed any party member was as free as a bird to make his views known.

In this febrile atmosphere Wilson made the mistake which was to put Callaghan at the exact point of balance in the party. He decided, and Roy Jenkins told the House, that the Government had resolved to introduce an early Bill in that session which would incorporate 'some of the more important provisions incorporated in the White Paper *In Place of Strife*'. This apparent haste aroused the usually torpid trade-union MPs from their lethargy. Already, union conference agendas were appearing with an avalanche of resolutions criticising the policy. One concession had been offered to them; there would be no new statutory controls over incomes. This in itself was a direct surrender to Callaghan and his Fire Brigades' Union speech. But it was not enough, because most trade unionists had assumed the controls would be dropped anyway. They began to scent victory.

It was at this time, with dismay spreading through the party, that Callaghan revealed a little of his approach. When Brian Walden, a back-bench Labour MP, pressed on him the view that union reform was 'inevitable', he replied 'O.K., if it's so inevitable, let the *Tories* pass it. All I'm saying is that it's not *our* issue.' And on 11 April, Victor Feather, General Secretary of the TUC, attacked the penal clauses of the proposed legislation for attempting to 'introduce the taint of criminality into industrial relations'. Ever one for the happy phrase, he added later 'Law courts do not make exports'. On these and other truisms Callaghan and the trade unionists based their arguments.

Callaghan's relationship with Wilson now entered a crucial phase. On 29 April 1969 Wilson included Callaghan in his 'inner cabinet'—a close-knit group of seven ministers who were supposed to work as a team and decide ultimate government strategy. Wilson's decision defied the confident predictions and urgent wishes of Callaghan's enemies; the Prime Minister evidently hoped that Callaghan would cause less trouble by toning down his arguments outside the Cabinet. Wilson, however, misjudged Callaghan's determination to press his case home.

By this time, it is important to note, Callaghan was the only senior Cabinet minister with any real trade-union connections. Both Ray Gunter and George Brown had taken themselves off in varying states of dudgeon, and Roy Mason, the Minister of Power, was the only other authentic proletarian at the top table.

As a result, Callaghan was able to maximise his role as 'the one who knows what the chaps in the unions think'.

His experience as Treasurer helped greatly. He became fond of telling people that, the previous February, he had addressed a meeting at Congress House and made the usual appeal for funds. The tone of the response was summed up by Danny McGarvey of the Boilermakers' Union, who said defiantly that any fines levied on trade unions would be deducted from the political funds which they maintained for the purpose of supporting the Labour Party. It was disquiet of this kind that had impelled even men like Tom Bradley, Roy Jenkins's Parliamentary Private Secretary and an official of the Transport Salaried Staffs Association, to vote against Castle in the National Executive Committee. With backing like that, Callaghan was unabashed at returning to the attack on 10 May, at a joint meeting between the Cabinet and the NEC. He spoke early in the meeting, arguing for a change of government policy which would heal the breach between the Government and the party in the country, and restore trade-union confidence. Wilson was furious. On 13 May he dropped Callaghan from the inner cabinet—just two weeks after appointing him—and came close to sacking him as Home Secretary. Callaghan was unmoved. 'On the very day that he was sacked from the inner cabinet', wrote Richard Crossman later, 'he sat beside the Prime Minister as though to emphasise that in opposing this measure he was fighting an ill-judged extremism and representing a middle road in which he had always believed and to which his colleagues would return after their moment of aberration.' And lest there should be any ambiguity, Callaghan made it plain to his press contacts ('his exploitation of trade union contacts and of the press during this period were also, for the experienced observer, a virtuoso performance', wrote Crossman) that he was not making any attempt to topple or replace Harold Wilson. He thus insured himself against any accusation of overt disloyalty. 'The Keeper of the Cloth Cap' had the resonance of a scornful joke when it was first coined for him, but it began to sound more and more like a compliment as time went on.

The TUC now drew up its battle plans. During May its General Council presented a *Programme for Action* which, while it made some concrete proposals about inter-union disputes, failed to satisfy Wilson or Castle about machinery for dealing with unofficial or 'unconstitutional' strikes. The TUC opted, on this crucial issue, for 'persuasion'. And it decided to make the entire offer of policing conditional on the dropping of the penal clauses. Moreover it called a special conference for 5 June to vote on the proposals. In the meantime, the TUC argued doggedly that the whole Castle package was born and conceived of the wrongheaded attitude that trade unionism was the enemy. The 5 June special conference, swayed by arguments like this and inflamed at the idea of statutory penalties, decided on a card vote by nearly eight million to just under one million to endorse the General Council's *Programme*.

The Government—or rather the people who followed the official government line—reacted with unrestrained ferocity. A government press statement roasted the TUC for avoiding the issue of enforcing discipline on unofficial strikers. Wilson told an after-dinner audience that trade-union irresponsibility was the same as that of the press lords. And the tone of Castle's and Healey's speeches turned from wheedling to bullying: they began to appear on platforms together, and both played their strongest and most traditional card—the Tories. 'If we did surrender', said Healey on 14 June, 'the British people would kick us out. Then you would have a Tory Government hell-bent on crippling trade unionism. That is the price the trade unions will have to pay.'

Callaghan meanwhile was becoming more emollient. Speaking on the same day as Healey, he contented himself with rebutting a claim, made by Dr Zijlstra of the Bank for International Settlements, that British industry was tinged with anarchy.

But the trade unions continued to play *their* strongest card—stubbornness—and not even all the rhetoric of Barbara Castle at her most impassioned could shift them. The feedback to the Parliamentary Labour Party was now so strong that on 17 June the Liaison Committee (a back-bench body supposed to keep lines open between the Government and its supporters) decided that the gap between the TUC and the Cabinet should not grow big enough to risk wrecking the party. They told Robert Mellish, the Chief Whip, of their view, and he attended a special Cabinet meeting that night. (He was not a full Cabinet member.) There Wilson and Castle gave their opinion, which was that the TUC's proposals were hopelessly feeble and that the legislation would have to go through.

The axe then fell. Mellish broke into the discussion to say that as Chief Whip he must advise the Cabinet that there would be no majority in Parliament for the penal clauses, and he could not answer for the party in the lobbies. Before his eyes, Wilson saw the Cabinet unravel, with Edward Short, Peter Shore, Cledwyn Hughes, Roy Mason and even Roy Jenkins throwing their sponges in. Callaghan, who sat quietly in the meeting, intervened at the end to affirm his loyalty on condition that Wilson would sue for peace with the TUC.

The following day, a face-saving formula was agreed and announced. The *Programme for Action* was accepted in a 'solemn and binding' fashion by all parties, and the TUC agreed to 'take energetic steps to obtain an immediate resumption of work including action within their rules' when strikers were thought to be harming the agreed conventions. But the decision on intervention was—crucially—to be left to the TUC. There would be no mandatory or automatic machinery, and no statutory penalties. Callaghan and his co-thinkers had won game, set and match. Douglas Houghton, who had played an important role as sounder-out of party opinion, might have felt a glow of pride as he recalled securing Callaghan his job at the Inland Revenue Staff Federation 33 years earlier. His protégé was now the broker of the party and the movement.

Barbara Castle never forgave Callaghan, and they have remained enemies ever since. One of his first acts as Prime Minister was to drop her from his Cabinet. But Wilson did forgive him. In October 1969 he restored Callaghan to the inner cabinet. He had, really, no choice but to do so. Callaghan had not pressed home his triumph with any leadership bid—he had kept his word there. And it was clearly unwise to exclude the minister responsible for law and order, immigration and Northern Ireland, from the most important councils of the Government.

Richard Crossman's subsequent observation in the *New Statesman* was probably the shrewdest: 'Once the anchor man had put his team clean out of the contest, he was prepared to collaborate loyally with them . . . one of the reasons Mr Callaghan survived the breaking of so many Cabinet conventions was his handling of the Ulster crisis. When his relations with No. 10 were at their worst, he was at long last providing an indispensable example of Labour's power to grapple with a major international crisis. In British politics a success which redounds on the whole government will atone for the most peculiar interpretation of collective responsibility and personal loyalty.'

Certainly Callaghan's reputation did rise with his handling of Ulster. Whether it deserved to, however, is another matter.

10

1967–73
The Children of God:
James Callaghan and
Ulster

'This is not a last chance for Ulster', I said, 'it is a great opportunity. Everyone in Ulster must face the fact that we are all children of God and everyone is entitled to and should receive an equal chance of a decent life.'
JAMES CALLAGHAN in *A House Divided*

'The moment the very name of Ireland is mentioned, the English seem to bid adieu to common feeling, common prudence, and common sense.'
SYDNEY SMITH in *Peter Plymley's Letters*

Callaghan once remarked of Chancellors that they fall into one of two categories—those who fail and those who get out in time. The same is now said of those luckless politicians who take on the job of administering the snake-pit of Northern Ireland. Having, as Chancellor, fallen heavily into the first category, Callaghan became the first and probably the last British politician to look better at the end of his stint on the Irish question than he had done at the beginning. But he was lucky, and the consequences of his shortcomings have been borne by the ministers who came after him.

When Callaghan became Home Secretary in November 1967, Ulster was still relatively quiet, enjoying—or suffering—local autonomy under an entrenched Protestant Government at Stormont Castle. The major clashes between civil rights demonstrators and the police did not begin until October 1968, but after that Callaghan presided over a steadily worsening crisis, culminating in British troops being sent to the province in August 1969 to try to restore peace. Internment, direct rule and the various ill-fated attempts to close the province's political schisms, all came after Labour left office in June 1970.

As Callaghan's own book, *A House Divided*, recalls, the Home Office staff dealing with Northern Ireland at the start of his term had been assimilated for years into the General Department, which covered such miscellaneous matters as London taxicabs, British Summer Time and state-owned pubs in Carlisle. After the first bout of political rioting in Londonderry in October 1968, Callaghan appointed precisely one civil servant allocated full-time to the Ulster problem, a decision which did not sound any firm note of authority. Yet authority was what Callaghan claimed to provide. As the affairs of the province started to deteriorate, he began to regard the crisis as his personal responsibility and one where, unlike the arid atmosphere of the Exchequer, his own brand of popular and human style could be deployed to the fullest effect. He writes (in *A House Divided*) that 'Harold Wilson personally gave me every encouragement throughout this period. Despite our earlier differences on the Industrial Relations Bill, he was kindness itself. He later told me that he regarded it as a turning point in the standing of the Labour Government, for we appeared to be handling an unprecedented situation with firmness and authority.'

For Callaghan, Ulster was the road back to personal self-confidence and political esteem. But in the long perspective with which Irishmen view their political history, his tenure has left little, if any, distinctive mark.

When Callaghan started dealing with the Ulster problem there were three interlocking problems to be faced and solved. The first and most immediate was the withdrawal of allegiance to the state by an increasing number of Catholics, who simply did not see the police and security forces as impartial or trustworthy. The second was the feeling of impending betrayal among the Protestant Loyalist community, who suspected that the mother country would do a deal behind their backs and set their loyalty at naught.

The third—and subsequently the overriding—problem was the threat of widespread sectarian violence.

Faced with this appalling triad, Callaghan can now be seen to have lost the initial trust of the Catholics, further alienated the Protestants and applied the wrong proportions of military and political intervention to the prospect of violence. Yet it did not seem that way at the time. To distinguish reputation from reality it is important to understand Callaghan's extraordinary facility with very ordinary people. The apparent ordinariness of voters and workers in the ghettos of Northern Ireland was, of course, deceptive, and masked the most remarkable set of political and national obsessions in modern Europe. But to Callaghan they were all children of God, all as it were potential constituents with shortages to be met and grievances to be smoothed over. Paddy Devlin recently recalled the impact Callaghan had on the Falls Road. 'He has a great smile and a great wave and a great way of approaching people . . . the crowds came from everywhere to see Callaghan . . . and the atmosphere was dead right because he represented everything that was totally different from the sort of politicians that we'd met before that. We did have difficulty getting him out of the Falls Road at the time . . . I would think that no one could sort of take away Callaghan's performance on that occasion. He did a marvellous job'.

For the beleaguered Catholics of Belfast and Londonderry, Callaghan was indeed the first politician they had met who seemed to regard them as equal citizens.

At this time the Cameron Commission, an inquiry into the 1968 disturbances, had not yet reported, but when it did it was widely expected to contain stern and shocking evidence about the sectarian behaviour of the Royal Ulster Constabulary. With his excellent police contacts, Callaghan was able to increase and overhaul the quality of leadership in the constabulary. But as he writes in his book, 'We tended to forget that one of the reasons why the Catholics so disliked the police was that they saw them as an arm of the Ulster Unionist Party.'

Having stumbled upon this truth, Callaghan picked himself up as if nothing had happened. The 'we' above refers to himself and Billy Blease, leader of Ulster's trade-union movement. For Callaghan, it was essentially a problem of trade-union negotiation—a concession here, a firm stand there, the occasional reward. A time for tough talking and a time to be bland. His book is littered with phrases like 'raising the temperature', 'lowering the temperature', 'lessening of tension', 'heightening of tension', 'unity' and 'division'.

It was not enough. His own book provides the evidence that it was not just a matter of keeping all the balls in the air at the same time. Discussing a conversation he had with Sam Napier, a leader of the Northern Ireland Labour Party, Callaghan recalls that he thought it 'a fair criticism' when Napier accused the Protestants of regarding 'the State and all its institutions as their own property'. This, indeed, was the root of the matter. Yet it was left to a later Conservative Government to bow to the inevitable and accept Direct Rule as the only short-term solution short of withdrawal. Callaghan consistently put off decisions about this crucial question, as he did over the commitment of troops. The critical moment came on 12 August 1969.

A restless Catholic population in Londonderry was appalled that the Apprentice Boys March would be permitted to proceed that year through the city as if nothing had happened since 1689. Delegations of shopkeepers and other worthy citizens visited the then Minister of Home Affairs, Robert Porter, as early as 25 July to warn him of the logical and probable results of permitting the march on 12 August. Porter himself attempted to persuade the march organisers to cancel. The senior members of the new Derry Development Commission did the same. But the leaders of the Unionist Party, and their then Prime Minister, Major James Chichester-Clark, decided on 11 August to let the parade go ahead. They were reassured in this by the fact that Callaghan had told them they could have British troops for a 'short, sharp, peacekeeping operation' if necessary, and they could have them without surrendering any part of their constitution of Northern Ireland. In effect, the British Government would let them borrow the army. From that decision came most, if not all, of the unravelling since. As the 12 August confrontation approached, the number of soldiers in the province was actually reduced, against the pleadings of the then GOC, General Freeland. (Some British troops had always been garrisoned in Ulster, as a United Kingdom province, on standard military duties.)

As far back as August 1966, Wilson, Callaghan and Terence O'Neill (the then Prime Minister of Northern Ireland) had discussed the terms of a military intervention. It was not, however, until two years later that the first full-time civil servant for Ulster affairs was gazetted. And, astonishingly, when the killing and looting began in August 1969, and it dawned on politicians that there was a limit to the effectiveness of walkabouts and inter-denominational banquets, there was still no contingency plan for the deployment of troops.

Callaghan's own change of mind on the use of the army is striking. Describing July 1969 and the violence which pre-figured the massive civil disturbances of the next month, he writes that 'The advice that came to me from all sides was on no account to get sucked into the Irish bog. For the time being we decided we would wait.' Then, a matter of weeks later, with all his conciliation schemes in ruins, with the police force worn down to a resentful rump on the blazing streets, and with no alternative but intervention, he acted very differently. Here is the account he gives of the days when the troop commitment to Ireland was made:

'In August 1969 the situation required me to exercise real authority, to do it quickly or be swamped ... It was a most unenviable position for any politician to be in: the Cabinet was on holiday, Harold Wilson was back in the Scillies, Parliament was not in session, and there was I in charge, pulling levers here, pushing levers there, saying get this, fetch so-and-so, and the whole machine absolutely buzzed.'

The boyish enthusiasm does not quite conceal the revelation that so far from dictating events, from saying to a man go and he goeth, Callaghan was in fact reacting to them, and reacting in a very pragmatic and short-term fashion.

The army's hasty arrival on the streets—the most extensive military commitment made by the British Government since the Second World War—began badly. Initially despatched to Derry, they did not arrive in Belfast until the RUC had earned the hatred of the Catholics of that city by using armoured cars in confined spaces.

But the store of Catholic goodwill for the Callaghan programme was not yet used up. The crucial issue on which it foundered was the one which he avoided. Now that the British Army was conducting 'duties in aid of the civil power', exactly who was the civil power to be? By leaving Stormont as the final authority in the province with its built-in Unionist majority, and by using the troops as the enforcers of the final authority, Callaghan ensured that sooner or later people would begin to associate the two things with each other.

Yet, while doing very little to allay the fears of Catholics about British troops being the property of the Unionist Party, Callaghan had not won the trust of the Protestants either. Brian Faulkner, who was the last Prime Minister of Northern Ireland, put it as tactfully as he could in a recent interview where he said that 'To be fair from the Unionist point of view, the people felt that he identified overmuch with the other side of the argument, what in those days was probably called the Civil Rights side of the argument.'

Although the Unionist leadership had fought a stiff rearguard action on making too many concessions, when the rioting got out of hand they were all too willing to accept the British Army. As Captain Lawrence Orr, Unionist leader at Westminster and head of the Orange Order, remarked in mid-August 1969, 'We're getting the troops. And we're getting them without strings.' It was this kind of comment which caused younger ministers concerned with the problem, among them Roy Hattersley, who had liaised with Callaghan from the Ministry of Defence, to urge that the Stormont Government should on no account be lent the British Army on a short-term basis.

After the troops had arrived, too few and too late, the Callaghan honeymoon with Ulster was soon enough over. He did tour the burned-out areas of Belfast, but there was no further point in 'meet the people' sessions. Things began to fall apart very quickly. On 3 October 1969, he spoke to the House of Commons about the progress of political reform in the province. To the horror of the Catholics, he made no mention of the need to overhaul or replace the Stormont Parliament. One colleague complained that Callaghan gave the impression of only objecting to the fact that the wrong party got elected. The other projected reforms—notably those touching upon slum housing and local government discrimination—were scheduled to take place at civil service tempo, involving years of gradual amelioration rather than the rapid change which Catholic leaders thought they had been told to expect. Once again, Paddy Devlin recalls, 'it's fairly obvious that the ground wouldn't have been as fertile for the para-militaries afterwards' if Callaghan had made 'some serious effort to mount a campaign to improve the areas as far as prosperity would be concerned'. And, it might be added, if Stormont had not been the filter through which all initiative passed. That winter 7 per cent of the working population was unemployed (12 per cent in Derry) and the high hopes started to recede.

Two other small, or apparently small, incidents illustrated the Government's insensitivity. A Cabinet feeling that proportional representation for elections (since implemented for Ulster polling) might make for a fairer distribution of the franchise was quashed by Callaghan's Home Office deputy Shirley Williams on the grounds that the Liberal Party would make domestic capital out of it. And Unionist Attorney General Basil Kelly proposed the abolition of all but the most reserve provisions of the Special Powers Act, a piece of legislation which had aroused fear and loathing among Catholics for years. For some reason he has never explained, Callaghan refused the offer, which was almost the only concession ever to come from the Unionists voluntarily. Both Kelly and Callaghan would have retained the power of internment, but the Kelly proposal would have symbolically cut away a long heritage of sectarian legislation.

By this time, the Protestants were losing patience. In September 1969 had come the Cameron report, which spelled out the need for reform while analysing the violence of the previous autumn in Derry. Then, in October, came a report by Lord Hunt on the police force, calling for the disarming of the RUC and the integration of Catholics into the police authority. A British senior officer, Sir Arthur Young, was to take over as chief officer. And the B-Specials (ill-disciplined Protestant special constables) were, as Loyalists had long feared, to be disbanded. On the night of 11 October, the Shankill Road saw deaths on both sides as Protestant rioters fought it out with the army and police. That exchange, and the revival of militant Orange parades which it presaged, were followed the next Easter by vicious rioting between troops and the Catholic inhabitants of the Ballymurphy housing estate. The riots brought Irish Republicans and British soldiers into armed conflict for the first time in generations. Callaghan wrote: 'We did not know it at the time, but those riots marked the emergence of the Provisional IRA as a separate force.'

It was, of course, impossible to please everybody. But as the above sequence shows, the Callaghan policy was enough to enrage the Protestants without getting them to agree enough concessions to pacify the Catholics. And, by this time, the Labour Government was in its dying days.

Since 1970 Callaghan has been extremely scathing at times about the performance of his successor, Reginald Maudling. He felt that Maudling left day-to-day affairs in the hands of the Unionists and the security forces, and undid the good work of his own tenure by permitting events like the Falls Road curfew, which finally ruptured all rapprochement between the army and the Catholic minority. But as Callaghan's own evidence shows, the gestation of the Provisional IRA had taken place under his own stewardship of affairs, and the record makes clear that he was lucky to have left office before the next autumn's 'marching season' began.

It is true that, impressed by the Treasury's 'contingency planning' for devaluation, Callaghan had drawn up a three-clause bill for the imposition of direct rule from Westminster. It is still not clear why the plan was not put into effect by Labour (who had nothing to lose from the end of Unionist ascendancy). Various explanations have been privately put forward. The first is a logistic one, which involves civil servants quailing at the prospect of having to take over and run a potentially hostile Ulster bureaucracy, and generals unwilling to commit such large numbers of troops. The figure mentioned was 15,000—unthinkable then, but the number that have normally been involved since. An alternative account, which has been admitted to close friends by William Whitelaw, suggests that the Tories would have seized the chance to accuse Labour of 'selling out' in the face of violence. This theory, which has some impressive precedents, says in effect that just as only de Gaulle could have abandoned French

Algeria, and only Richard Nixon could have begun withdrawal from Vietnam, reforming parties dare not risk the odium which attaches to such national traumas. The most likely explanation, given the relatively bloodless and determined way in which the Conservative Government did proceed to outface the Unionists and instal direct rule, is that the only thing lacking was political will.

In opposition, Jim Callaghan did not seem disposed to do any more than follow events either. At the Labour Conference later that year, he opposed resolutions and speeches calling for direct rule, and on other occasions spoke out against the wisdom of having a British minister permanently responsible for the province. (Though, when such a job became necessary, he was happy and pleased to secure it both as shadow and as reality for his friend Merlyn Rees.)

When internment came in August 1971, Callaghan gave it a guarded and tacit welcome. He has since denied that he was told of it in advance, but some of his colleagues have memories to the contrary. At any event, as soon as it became clear that internment had not worked in reducing the level of violence (August was the first month in which violent bomb explosions topped the hundred mark, and there were nearly ten times as many deaths as during the previous month) he was equal to the task of saying that it had not worked. He did not go so far as saying that it should end, because once it had been started it was difficult to release anybody, but he did point out that some people had been undeservedly arrested. Once again, he was content to shadow events.

The same caution and even banality can be found in the book *A House Divided* which describes his tour of duty in Ulster and which he published in 1973. Callaghan is proud of the book—and of the effort it took to prepare it: he once told a BBC interviewer that 'the book I wrote on Northern Ireland was literally torn out of me'. The man who did the 'tearing' was John Clare, who had covered much of the same ground in Ulster for *The Times*. He was asked to help by Callaghan, and taped two hours of solid reflection twice a week for several months. Having started out on the project with enthusiasm and interest, Clare now says that he rapidly became disappointed. The book does not cover any but the most well-trodden ground, and apart from a few personal anecdotes it is barren of revelation. Large parts of it give the effect of having been written for Callaghan, and this combined with the effects of tape-recording may account for the many repetitions, if not some of the apparent contradictions, in his narrative. At the end of the arrangement, Clare wrote to Callaghan hinting at his lack of enthusiasm and offering to waive the balance of £1,000 which was to be paid to him on completion. Clare had already received £500. Callaghan's reply thanked him for all his help—and accepted the waiver.

When it came to formulating conclusions, Clare says that to his surprise Callaghan asked for his views on what they ought to be. The former minister seemed to Clare to have none of his own, and the rather woolly endorsement of ultimate Irish reunification stems, in Clare's view, from a temperamental attachment to and preference for the word 'unity' (as against the dreaded 'division').

There is, however, one final hostage to fortune in the text. On the penultimate page, Callaghan says that 'If, at any time, the Assembly and the Executive should be made unworkable through a deliberate refusal by the majority to play their part, then in my judgement the United Kingdom would be entitled to reconsider her position and her pledges on all matters . . . so if, by sabotage of the political structure of the Northern Ireland, the majority deliberately contracted out, then Britain should feel morally free to reconsider the link between herself and Northern Ireland, the provision of troops to Northern Ireland and the financial subsidy to the Province.'

When the Ulster Executive was brought down two years later by political and industrial action against power-sharing, it must have occurred to many people that Ulster was no longer a problem to be handled by alternate stick and carrot, by bluff and jovial dealing, or by military rule. It may well be that no British politician will ever be able to devise an Irish solution. If that maxim turns out to be true, James Callaghan was one of the first to demonstrate its efficacy.

11

1970–4
How to Consolidate
a Power Base

'In any battle between bureaucracy and charisma, the tactical advantages of bureaucracy are generally decisive.'

MAX WEBER

The June 1970 Election defeat left the Labour Party confused and demoralised. Although many MPs privately blamed Callaghan for torpedoing *In Place of Strife*, he was not very greatly hampered in the task he now set himself inside the party. This was to use his peculiar skills in reconstructing the PLP–Trade Union–Constituency tripod, which was by this time rather battered. At the first post-election PLP meeting Callaghan took the chair, replied to the discussion in Wilson's stead and struck his unity note, not for the first time.

One month later, with Jenkins overwhelmingly elected as Deputy Leader (beating Michael Foot and humiliating Fred Peart), Callaghan easily defeated Barbara Castle and Ian Mikardo for the post of Chairman of the Home Policy Sub-Committee of the NEC. He also came first in the elections for the PLP's Parliamentary Committee, from which the shadow cabinet is drawn; Callaghan became shadow Home Secretary. Straight away, he made it clear that while he might have allied with the left on union legislation, he was in no sense in their debt. 'If you want a Front Bench of neutered tabby cats', he told them at one meeting, 'you can count me out.'

As in Labour's previous period of opposition before 1964, Callaghan was consistently successful in both parliamentary and national party elections, where he held off the challenge of the Tribune MP Norman Atkinson for the treasurership:

	PARLIAMENTARY COMMITTEE		TREASURER	
			Callaghan	Atkinson
	votes	*place*		
1970	178	1	3,860,000	2,225,000
1971	134	4	3,646,000	2,536,000
1972	142	5	3,575,000	2,624,000
1973	150	1	3,492,000	2,568,000

With figures like these, Callaghan assured himself of a central role in reviving the Labour Party, and determining its tactics for opposing the Conservative Government.

Shortly after the 1970 Election the Conservatives declared their hand on several crucial issues involving major legislation. On trade unions, their Industrial Relations Bill was clearly going to be based on the early provisions of their 1968 policy document *Fair Deal at Work*, with special emphasis on the registration of unions and the closed shop. On immigration, they proposed severe restrictions on entry, based in part on Callaghan's own concept of 'patriality'. And the centrepiece of their strategy and of the Heath leadership emerged, predictably, as one of consummating Britain's relationship with the European Economic Community. Callaghan's instinct was to respond to all these policies with caution; but on immigration his hand was forced by the left.

At the NEC meeting in December 1970, a resolution came from Callaghan's own fief at the Home Policy Committee, noting the recommendations of the European Commission on Human Rights, which attacked Labour's 1968 immigration measures. The resolution called for the issue of unused entry vouchers to alleviate the hardship of stateless people holding British passports. Callaghan, who apologised for not having been at the Home Policy Committee which had drawn up this resolution, launched a fierce attack on the idea and argued that it would be disastrous for Labour to become associated with further immigration. He argued for the resolution to be referred back for reconsideration. But Shirley Williams countered him strongly by pointing out that Labour could not delay having a policy until the Tories introduced their new Bill. She said that many members of the

Government had only voted for the 1968 Act because of Callaghan's verbal assurance that those who were deprived of employment and expelled from East Africa would not be turned away (see p. 80). His motion for a reference back was defeated, even though most of the trade union members voted for it. Callaghan replied bitterly that the party had hung an albatross around its neck.

He then left the meeting early. By doing so he avoided voting on another sensitive issue: whether to hold a special conference of the Labour Party on the Common Market. In just the same way, he had absented himself from an earlier meeting which had decided who should represent Labour on the pro-Market Monnet Committee.) 'I'm keeping my powder dry', he remarked cryptically to one friend.

The Immigration Bill continued to make Callaghan's life as shadow Home Secretary difficult in the early months of 1971. At the shadow cabinet on 3 March, Harold Wilson proposed that Jenkins, the man with impeccable libertarian credentials, should wind up the debate on the Bill, and was greeted with a chorus of 'hear hear'. Callaghan was put out by the suggestion, and mentioned that Merlyn Rees (his own former Home Office deputy), would also be disappointed. Then Shirley Williams followed up her earlier triumph at the NEC by asking what the party line would be on the 'patrial' issue. At this, Callaghan began to expostulate. 'I know what is going on,' he said, 'there is a small group, and Shirley is part of it, who disagreed with my line in 1968. I can't go back on what I said about the patrial clause.' He then astonished the newly elected members of the shadow cabinet, in particular Michael Foot, by saying: 'I wonder if the party shouldn't get someone else to conduct the Bill.' Wilson hastily said that there would be unwelcome public comment if Callaghan didn't speak at all, and eventually it was decided that he should do so, drawing a distinction between the Tory patrial clauses and his own.

While Callaghan suffered tactical embarrassment over immigration, he was achieving important strategic victories in the machinery of Labour policy-making. As chairman of the Home Policy Committee he was in a position to draw together Labour's MPs, local constituency parties, and the trade unions; and the way he used his authority helped Labour to avoid the kind of schisms which had afflicted the party in 1960.

Callaghan proposed that a series of study groups should be set up, to devise new policies for the next Labour Government. MPs, elected NEC members, and trade unionists would all be represented. Callaghan was not so much concerned with the *policies* they determined—except over nationalisation, which was to cause trouble later—as with the *activity* of policy-making as a means of preserving party unity. He did, however, take some care over the personnel of the groups. At an NEC meeting in February 1971, left-wingers noticed that the proposed lists of group participants leaned rather heavily towards the right. Castle proposed adding Eric Heffer to the industrial policy group to restore some balance; Callaghan opposed this with the ingenious argument that the parliamentary manpower for the groups should be drawn from the front bench—and Heffer was only on the front bench for the short-term purpose of opposing the Industrial Relations Bill. Callaghan won the argument in this case, but he was defeated on another occasion when Reginald Freeson was accepted for the social services group.

Callaghan carefully presented himself at this time as an impartial bridge-builder. To show he was no mere cipher for large union leaders, he wrote in January 1971 an article for the journal of the Amalgamated Union of Engineering Workers in which he called for trade-union acceptance of a Labour voluntary incomes policy. He argued his point as 'a personal view, put forward in the light of the experience of the past six years'. And, though he condemned the Industrial Relations Bill of Robert Carr, he added: 'It is indefensible that a handful of men, by withdrawing their labour, can put 2,000 of their fellows in the same factory out of work. Nor is it in the spirit of trade unionism to fail to carry out agreements and procedures that have been freely entered into (and not many are made under coercion today).' These comments aroused some cynicism among those who had supported *In Place of Strife*, but they restored Callaghan's friendship with Wilson, and as trade-union antagonism to the Conservative proposals became more and more determinedly militant, many MPs were prepared to grant what they would not have granted Callaghan two years before—that there were limits beyond which the TUC could not and should not be pushed.

Although Callaghan remained shadow Home Secretary until April 1972, he continued to stray from his departmental concerns. As we noted in Chapter 4, the distribution of power and influence inside the Labour Party depends greatly on whether the party is in government or opposition. In opposition, the patronage of the leader is less important (not least because the Parliamentary Committee is elected by MPs), and the influence of the party outside Parliament is greater. Callaghan's standing both among MPs, and in the NEC, meant that he had a freedom to say what he wanted on subjects he chose, which he never had in 1964–70. (Even over *In Place of Strife*, he was careful not to breach *publicly* the doctrine of collective cabinet responsibility.)

With his new freedom, Callaghan calculated where his most important contribution to party policy-making lay. As 1971 progressed, it became increasingly clear what course he had chosen: he would take a firm public stance against the Common Market; moreover, he would make this issue the theme of his rehabilitation with the three wings of the party. Not only that, he would try to make the Common Market one of Labour's chief selling points against the Conservatives. It was to be Jim in his favourite role of 'honest broker'; and if he succeeded it would benefit both the party and himself.

His first use of the word 're-negotiation' (a helpful term supplied to him by his son-in-law Peter Jay) did not occur until the end of 1971 (at Bradford). Jay saw it as an elastic device for obscuring Labour's divisions while rearranging an ordered withdrawal, but Callaghan seized on it as a way of giving his own strategy an apparent consistency. His instincts were undoubtedly hostile to the EEC; the point is that he subordinated these to a political calculation that the Labour Party might well require diametrically opposed policies in opposition and in government.

But it was as early as May 1971 that he developed the strategy of criticising the Common Market without opposing it; of entering caveats and reservations without calling for outright rejection of entry; of denouncing the terms and the Tory method of negotiation without being (or needing to be) too specific about Labour's own alternatives.

On 25 May, at the Bitterne Park School in Southampton, he turned a run-of-the-mill by-election meeting into a national tribune from which to launch his campaign. Television and newsmen were informed in advance, somewhat to the astonishment of local Labour stalwarts who found the hall festooned with lights and cameras. In the much-publicised climax to his speech he said: 'Millions of people in Britain have been surprised to hear that the language of Chaucer, Shakespeare and Milton must in future be regarded as an American import from which we must protect ourselves if we are to build a new Europe. We can agree that the French own the supreme prose literature in Europe. But if we are to prove our Europeanism by accepting that French is the dominant language in the Community, then the answer is quite clear, and I will say it in French to prevent any misunderstanding: *Non, merci beaucoup.*'

It was an atmospheric masterpiece. In his Southampton speech, Callaghan raised all the misgivings about food prices, undue continental influences, and the loss of old Commonwealth friends, which formed the subconscious feelings of reservation about 'Greater Europe'. He achieved the calculated effect of defining both the tone and the parameters of the debate to come.

At the National Executive meeting of 23 June 1971 he made his next move. He surprised the left by supporting their call for a special party conference on the EEC. Puzzled by his earlier inscrutability on the issue, the left had called for a purely consultative 'no vote' conference, which would not bind passionate believers on either side of the argument. They thought this stood the best chance of winning over waverers to the anti-Market cause without doing too much violence to party unity; the PLP at that time being split 140–140 on the issue. Of course, Callaghan knew as well as other old warriors, like Mikardo, that once a conference was convened it could make its own rules of procedure and take a vote if it so wished. But he voted with the anti-Market bloc, and the date of 17 July was duly set.

In the interval between the NEC meeting and the special conference, Harold Wilson had a meeting with some of his staff. Drawing a few of them to one side, he produced pen and envelope and demonstrated to them by means of a rough flow diagram that the ambitious Callaghan would purport to lead the party away from Europe while actually preparing the ground for a consolidation of Britain's role (under Labour) in the 're-negotiated' EEC. One of those present at the meeting has told us that Wilson anticipated every step of the subsequent 'endgame' brought off by the Labour leadership. But the credit for it goes to Jim.

On 4 July, two weeks before the conference, Callaghan gave the anti-Market case in the *Sunday Mirror*. His theme was that Heath's obsession with Europe had panicked voters into accepting the view that there was no alternative to joining the Common Market. This he rejected with gusto. 'Britain is not finished if we stay out of Europe', he wrote. 'We still have a choice. There is another road.' He stressed the Commonwealth and called for a policy of economic growth, in contrast to the much-criticised Roy Jenkins who was known both as strongly pro-Market and as the ex-Chancellor who had denied growth in his 1970 Budget.

At the conference itself, Callaghan spoke early in the proceedings. On behalf of the NEC he successfully argued that there should be no resolution taken which would anticipate the party's October annual conference. And in the little time left to him, he spelt out his abiding strategy for the battle. 'It is our desire, and the National Executive's plan on this matter is laid out in such a way as to preserve the maximum unity of the Party, to ensure that we are able to go to the people of the country as soon as is necessary, having preserved our unity, in order to get rid of the Conservative Government and to settle the account on behalf of the British people.' For this purpose, it was essential that the Labour Party did not adopt an uncompromising anti-Market stand at an early stage or, indeed, adopt such a stand at all. It was of this devious stratagem that Harold Macmillan remarked: 'I always knew they'd rat. It was the same in the thirties. They were for rearmament, *but not under Baldwin.*'

Meanwhile, a large minority of the Parliamentary Labour Party had clearly said that they would vote with the neo-Baldwin, Heath, on what they considered an issue of principle. It was a fraught time for the party. Men who understood the workings and rhythms of party unity were going to be at a premium, and Callaghan could offer unrivalled skills in that department. He resented any allegation to the contrary.

On 23 July, only a week after the special conference, Callaghan wrote a private note to Alan Watkins, political correspondent of the *New Statesman*. Watkins had reported that Callaghan was taking great umbrage at the active pro-Market stance of Roy Jenkins. 'You are wrong in saying that I was "padding the corridors on Monday night telling everyone who would listen about the shocking thing that Mr Jenkins had just done"', wrote Callaghan. 'As a matter of fact, I went off home and spoke to hardly anybody. As you certainly did not see me last Monday night, I can only wonder who the mischief maker is on whom you relied.' Watkins offered to publish a correction, and was surprised to receive the following: 'I certainly do not wish you to put the correct version of this matter in your column, although for your information let me say that throughout the whole Common Market business I have had three objectives. One is to keep us out of the Market, the second is to get rid of the Tory government and the third is to preserve party unity. So you are quite wrong in assuming that it was a likely thing for me to be padding round the corridors complaining about Roy.'

In September 1971, Callaghan launched a fresh programme of speeches on the Market theme, all of them directed at the 'terms' which the Heath Government was about to settle under the Treaty of Rome. These terms, said Callaghan in a meeting at Bradford when he first began to introduce the re-negotiation element, were 'unfair and too stiff to accept'. He went on, 'Our aim is to persuade Parliament that it should not cast a vote in favour of Britain's entry *until better terms can be won* [our italics]. We can afford to wait,' said Callaghan; 'in this matter time is not on the side of the Community; time is on our side.' His respective home towns of Cardiff and Portsmouth heard speeches on the same lines that month, where he spelt out the triad of Labour objections—on the Community budget, the common agricultural policy and on tariffs.

By the time of the Labour Party's annual conference in October, Callaghan had carved out a spokesmanship for himself. He won an easy pre-conference triumph at the National Executive, where to the annoyance of Denis Healey it was agreed that Callaghan should make a long wind-up speech on the Europe debate, and that Healey should open it. In this speech, which was well received by the delegates, Callaghan compared Heath unfavourably to George Brown on the CAP terms, announced that the EEC was 'designed more in the interests of capital than labour' and demanded special protective protocols, such as those enjoyed by Italy, for the purpose of regional development. The EEC was, he said, a specious invitation to 'turn away from the open seas'.

Two resolutions at the conference were defeated on the advice of the NEC. One spoke of rejecting entry 'on any terms'. The other called for a referendum. His rear thus secured, Callaghan spoke in the House of Commons later in the month and declared that with the Tory procedure for Europe 'the first step in the long centuries of history in stripping itself of its power of independent decision over a large sector of national life' had been taken by the House of Commons.

In January 1972 Callaghan underwent an operation for the removal of a prostate gland. This particular piece of surgery is notoriously demoralising in its effects, and for a while close friends wondered if he might not abandon politics. But his morale recovered with his health; and the resignation, in April, of Roy Jenkins, Harold Lever and George Thomson from the shadow cabinet had a tonic effect. They disliked the entire trend of Labour's approach to the EEC, and their departure made Callaghan's own formula much more readily acceptable in the inner councils of the party. In the 'grass roots', too, the feeling was that whatever the view taken of the Market, Jenkins and his supporters were giving aid and comfort to the Tories. The subsequent re-shuffle saw Callaghan assuming the spokesmanship on Foreign Affairs, and he was able also to secure the job of shadow Northern Ireland Secretary for his friend and supporter Merlyn Rees.

Much of the rest of 1972 was taken up with the drafting of Labour's *Programme for Britain*, which Callaghan presented in October. It presaged the idea of a 'social contract' with the TUC as an alternative to the running battles then being waged between the Conservatives and the trade unions. Callaghan added to his union popularity at this time by supporting the TUC on its demand for a conciliation and arbitration service, and by departing from his brief when speaking on Labour's programme to look up and say that he personally agreed with the National Union of Mineworkers about the vital importance of indigenous fuel in the 1970s. The prophetic significance of this remark was hugely enhanced by the energy crisis from 1973 on, but even at the time Callaghan knew that the miners' victorious strike in early 1972 made them Labour's 'brigade of guards'.

The next month—November 1972—Callaghan doffed one of his four hats. He retired as chairman of the Home Policy Committee of the party in order to concentrate on his Treasurership, on his deputy chairmanship of the party and his new Foreign Affairs brief. But he remained a member of the committee, and kept in touch with its deliberations.

In the spring of 1973, as shadow Foreign Secretary, he teamed up rather ingloriously with Ian Mikardo, chairman of the party's International Committee, for a visit to South-East Asia, including both North and South Vietnam. The trip was not a success—apart from the fact that the two men do not get on together too well, Callaghan found most people in the area unresponsive to his brand of jocular and conciliatory talk. The fact that the British Government of Harold Wilson had supported Lyndon Johnson and Richard Nixon so unquestioningly in their war effort did not endear him to many neutralist politicians (or to the North Vietnamese); and the mere fact of their being in the Labour Party was enough to ensure that President Thieu did not allow the delegation access to South Vietnam's political prisons.

Journalists based in Saigon still recall with amazement the press conference that Callaghan gave towards the end of his tour. Asked his opinion of President Thieu, he replied that 'he would make a damn good member of Labour's National Executive'. 'Surely better than that, Mr Callaghan', said one of those present, at which the shadow Foreign Secretary threatened to walk out. He compared the South Vietnamese stand at Anh Loc to the heroism of Stalingrad—thus annoying both sides by his infelicity—and called for the recognition of the Communist forces by Britain—something that was not done until the day after they had won in 1975, by which time he was Foreign Secretary. The tour was not much noticed in Britain, which in the circumstances may have consoled him.

Two months later, in May 1973, Callaghan nearly left British politics altogether. He received an approach from the International Monetary Fund, which was looking for a managing director, at a salary of £20,000 per annum tax free. Callaghan showed enough interest for Giscard d'Estaing, then France's Finance Minister, to spend time ensuring that he never got it: Giscard feared Callaghan's strong opposition to the French dream of European economic and monetary union.

Roy Jenkins, who had previously declined the same offer without any French pressure, remarked rather unkindly to friends that the job had now been offered to so many people that it was beginning to seem like dirty laundry. But by June it was clear that Callaghan was out of the running, though at the time he announced that he had himself decided not to take the offer. Without French opposition, it is interesting to speculate as to what his decision might have been.

In the same autumn Callaghan faced the combined opposition of the Engineering and Transport Workers Unions in the now annual battle between himself and the left-wing MP Norman Atkinson, but had little difficulty in overcoming it. More serious was the tussle in which he became engaged with the group of intellectuals and trade unionists who had been given the job of drafting Labour's proposals for industry. An Industrial Policy Committee had met for the first time on 28 April 1971, and in the intervening two-and-a-half years met twenty-seven times. On only one occasion, in December 1971, had Callaghan used his membership of the committee to favour it with his presence. In early 1973 he discovered, as did Wilson, that this committee sought to bind the party to large-scale intervention in the 'sector leaders' of British industry—'the twenty-five companies' which came to constitute one definition of the famous 'commanding heights' of industry.

Like Callaghan, Wilson had taken little interest in the detailed policy-making by the groups set up after the 1970 election. Now he saw the need to intervene. Callaghan, who, according to NEC members, had previously been content to support any proposals the unions seemed to back, fell tactically in behind his leader. Although this seemed to run counter to the political tactics

E

Callaghan had pursued ever since the 1969 battles over *In Place of Strife*, a curious consistency can be discerned. Callaghan believes that two parallel rules must always be upheld. Labour must do nothing which will wreck its party base; and it must do nothing which will wreck its national support. *In Place of Strife*, he believed, would break the first rule; the 'twenty-five companies' plan would break the second.

Wilson wanted to unite the party behind a vague phrase rather than divide it over a specific commitment. He suggested 'controlling interest in relevant companies'—an echo of his 1964 phrase about 'industries which are failing the nation'. When the issue came before a special meeting of the NEC at the Churchill Hotel in the summer of 1973, Wilson sarcastically described the people who wanted to keep the 25-company commitment as socialists who 'plan to raise Marks and Spencer to the efficiency of the Co-op'. In the event, the left was prepared to concede the specific request to drop the twenty-five names, in return for promises not to dilute the concepts of a National Enterprise Board and planning agreements. The NEC approached the autumn party conference, if not united, then at least with the cracks well covered.

Shortly before the conference a squall blew up which threatened to destroy this compromise. A proposal came before the NEC at its October meeting which would commit Labour to re-nationalising the 'hived-off' parts of publicly owned industry which the Tories were engaged in returning to private enterprise (though by the time they left office they had not progressed far beyond Thomas Cook's and the famous pubs of Carlisle). Sidney Weighell of the National Union of Railwaymen proposed a 'no compensation' clause in order to deter asset-strippers and speculators from moving in and making a windfall profit at the public expense. The National Executive divided by 17 votes to 6 in his favour, and Callaghan was furious: he called the proposal 'legalised robbery'.

Although the NEC's decision was not formally reversed, Wilson and Callaghan insisted that it would form no part of any election manifesto. By allowing the left to keep its formal victory, but by denying them its logical consequences, Wilson and Callaghan succeeded in defusing a potentially awkward problem.

*

The whole debate was given added importance and vitality by the prospect of an early General Election, which Heath's 'Who rules Britain?' confrontation with the miners made more likely. To some extent this made Callaghan's argument with the 'theologians' easier. 'The days of debate about the election programme are now over. The time for decision has begun', he told the Labour Parliamentary Association. He proposed a 'short, pithy and hard-hitting' manifesto, to enable debate to focus on Tory short-comings rather than crystal-clear Labour proposals which could give the Government a lever for counter-attack. It was vintage Callaghan—the thing to do was get the vote out and keep the ranks closed. Ideological discussion was for the dog-days of opposition.

Once the February 1974 election campaign began, efforts by both parties to control the social and political temperature were momentarily torpedoed by Michael McGahey, the Communist leader of the Scottish mineworkers. Attacking the state of emergency decreed by the Tories to cope with the work to rule and then strike with which the miners had pressed their wage claim, he turned to the possibility of troops being used to break the stranglehold on the supply and movement of coal. He recalled the language of fifty years previously, when J. R. Campbell had issued a 'don't shoot' appeal to the armed forces and precipitated the collapse of the 1924 Labour Government. McGahey called on soldiers to disobey any such order in 1974, and to remember their working-class origins. It was perfectly intelligible to his militant miners' audience, but the Tories saw it as a golden opportunity to mobilise the middle-class vote against the Communist influence in the trade unions.

Callaghan acted with considerable speed and despatch. After a few hours spent cruising round the tea-rooms and corridors of the House of Commons he was able to report widespread rage and dismay amongst Labour MPs at this 'politicisation' of the miners' just cause. Callaghan's 'soundings' led to a motion on the order paper making the same points and signed almost immediately by more than 100 Labour MPs. He also persuaded Joe Gormley, President of the National Union of Mineworkers, to use his authority to attack McGahey. Gormley's statement was followed by an even stronger one from Callaghan and Wilson in which they 'utterly repudiated' the subversive character of McGahey's call. The Tory thrust was deflected almost before it had been delivered, and Callaghan took the credit for a tactical master-stroke.

As the election campaign gathered momentum, Callaghan as chairman of the party had great influence in the campaign committee. Bob Worcester, of Market & Opinion Research International, who advised Labour on poll findings and electoral strategy, remembers Callaghan at the morning meetings where questions of understanding and interpretation arose. 'Callaghan often asked the most perceptive questions,' he recalls, 'and one of them was "What would you do with this information if you were a Conservative?" which is one hell of a question.' Worcester also recalls a period from late 1973 through to early 1974 when all indications were that the Liberals were picking up support rapidly. He calculated that the alleged 'bandwagon' was drawing more support from former Conservative voters than it was from Labour ones. Thus, when Labour campaign planners asked at morning meetings 'What shall we do about the Liberals?', Worcester replied simply: 'Nothing.' Callaghan, he recalls, was quick to take this point—quicker than many of his colleagues. For him, this was the stuff of politics.

Callaghan, then, fought the February 1974 General Election having succeeded in becoming the most influential Labour politician after Wilson. His respect among MPs, his repeated victories in the treasurership elections, and his skill in handling the issue of the Common Market, all contributed to a growing belief that he could succeed Wilson as party leader.

The election campaign itself reinforced Callaghan's position. While the opinion polls showed persistent Conservative leads over Labour, Callaghan combined a shrewd understanding of how voters behaved with an astute assessment of Bob Worcester's poll findings. Partly under Callaghan's influence, Labour played down the constitutional implications of the miners' dispute, and played up inflation; by ignoring Jeremy Thorpe, the party gave the Liberals enough rope to hang the Conservatives; by skilfully deploying the Common Market issue, Labour won extra votes via the unexpected support of Enoch Powell. In his own speeches,

Callaghan's reassuring 'steady as she goes' style contrasted favourably with the strident, and sometimes even hysterical, appeals made by the Conservative leadership for the electorate to choose between them and anarchy.

With the three-day week and the rocketing price of oil undermining the economy, Callaghan's tactics were just right—and they just worked.

12

Callaghan, Wales and Julian Hodge

*. . . and then as if perceiving Hodge to be out of countenance, adding
"but he is a very fine cat, a very fine cat indeed".'*
JAMES BOSWELL, in *The Life of Dr Johnson*

In his rise to the top of Labour's tree, James Callaghan has by no
means escaped criticism, and many of the specific complaints
against him are to be found elsewhere in this book. But in general,
even his most devoted enemies have allowed him credit for a
sound constituency performance, a combination of the human
touch and political flair which has ensured the safety of his seat
by comfortable margins at all elections—with the exception of
that in 1959.

In recent years, however, he has suffered from persistent
references, part rumour and part fact, to his association with
certain Welsh business interests in particular and with a rather
hidebound and unpopular Welsh Labour Establishment in
general. During the debate on the much-disputed Labour
Government decision to shelve the report of the Boundaries
Commission, Callaghan was angry to hear the Tory MP Sir
David Renton say that 'if the Boundaries Commission's report
were accepted, it [Callaghan's constituency] would be entirely
inside the city of Cardiff'. He replied, 'The whole of my constituency, every single bit of it, is inside the city of Cardiff.' Renton
apologised, but also checked his facts and found them correct.
The following day (15 October 1969) Callaghan made a statement
in which he said, 'I owe the right honourable and learned member
for Huntingdon an apology for interrupting him last night to
challenge his statement that my constituency is partly inside and
and partly outside the City of Cardiff. He is, of course, right.' To

many of Callaghan's critics, such a light-minded attitude towards his home seat seems to be indicative of what is wrong with Welsh Labour's long hegemony over the working-class vote, and part of the explanation for its recent reverses—notably the shattering local election defeats of May 1976.

What might be loosely called gossip about Callaghan's private resources did not really begin until he became the owner of Upper Clayhill Farm, a 138-acre dairy and arable retreat near Lewes in Sussex. (It was withdrawn from auction at £20,000 shortly before he bought it in the spring of 1968.) But apart from the fact that he has had a private war with poisonous tree-creepers, and is always toting a pair of secateurs with which to undo their efforts, little is known about Callaghan's acquisition or management of the farm. It certainly added 'Farmer Jim' to his many other titles ('Stoker', 'Smiler', 'Officer') but this in itself only reinforced his genial and avuncular image by making it bucolic as well.

However, in the year of opposition 1972, Callaghan took two steps into the no-man's-land between British politics and British finance, where questions are always being asked but, thanks in part to the admirably imperturbable nature of our legal system, almost never answered. On 20 March 1972 he became a director of the Italian International Bank, a 'consortium bank' formed by four Italian bankers to deal in international money markets. Some cynicism was aroused by the essentially capitalist nature of his co-directors, among them Lord Cobbold, a man much festooned with directorships, and Sir Charles Forte of household fame. (Lord Cobbold was the former theatre censor highly praised by Callaghan when he was Home Secretary.) Callaghan stayed only thirteen months as a director, resigning in May 1973. That year's annual report records that the six directors were paid a total of £28,000, but it is not clear how much Callaghan himself received.

More interestingly, Sir Charles Forte subscribed £5,000 to the Commercial Bank of Wales, a 'fringe bank' launched in late May 1972. The board, which then included James Callaghan, George Thomas (now Speaker of the House of Commons) and Lord Harlech, was put together by Sir Julian Hodge, a Cardiff merchant banker knighted by Labour in 1970 'for services to Wales'. (Callaghan's directorship only lasted while he was in opposition:

no government minister is allowed to hold such commercial positions.)

Hodge had, indeed, been a lifelong supporter of and donor to the Labour Party. But questions about his relationship with Callaghan were raised (though, it must be stressed, there is no evidence of any impropriety on either side) when it was recalled: that in his 1967 budget Callaghan relaxed the hire-purchase restrictions on three-wheeled cars, one of the chief manufacturers of which was Reliant Motors, a Hodge subsidiary; that Hodge took Callaghan to meetings of the International Monetary Fund as a guest after he had ceased to be Chancellor; and that in 1971 Callaghan had proposed to the Labour Party Conference a fund-raising idea involving a motor insurance scheme, which might well have enriched the party but would also have enriched the Hodge Group, whose insurance was the brand under offer. Alf Allen of the Shop-Workers' Union moved the reference back of the proposal in closed session; with support from the Co-op Insurance, who had traditionally enjoyed a monopoly in such matters, a card vote defeated Treasurer Callaghan by a margin of nearly three millions—a much more decisive defeat than he was accustomed to.

Julian Hodge's business ethic was not to everybody's taste, though there was nothing illegal about it. Granada Television devoted an entire programme to his links with a 'pyramid selling' operation, known as 'Holiday Magic'. In 1972 alone hundreds of mainly immigrant and coloured families were brought to or beyond the verge of financial ruin by 'pyramid selling' (still then within the law) which recruited gullible salesmen and women to peddle cosmetics. The inducement was the right or chance to earn a possible thousand pounds or more per month (then worth a great deal more than it would be today). The inevitable catch was the thousand or more pounds required to 'buy in' to the Holiday Magic franchise in the first place.

It was a combination of hard sell and easy lend, originating with an American company, but fuelled by money lent by the Hodge Group. The formula can be set down in a few words. First, a door-to-door representative would call at selected households, offering the chance to break out of the trivial round and the common task, into big money. If the 'prospect' seemed to be agreeable to the idea, an independent finance agent or broker would follow up the 'prospect', to arrange the necessary loan (in the region of one thousand pounds) so that the lucky householder could pay the 'Holiday Magic' starting price. In the majority of cases, the loan would be supplied by Julian Hodge's bank in Cardiff, and the security would take the form of a second mortgage on the applicant's own home. This was watertight enough from the Hodge point of view, in that default of payment by the borrower would mean that the bank could sell his home. The interest rates charged to borrowers were by no means paltry, but then neither was the original financial inducement. Many hundreds of families fell for it.

At the end of 1973, pyramid selling was made illegal by the Conservative Government; the new law, together with the inherent instability of the pyramid selling system, meant that many clients of the operation were left with their dream of super-salesmanship unfulfilled. To be exact, some of them had failed to sell so much as a single lipstick. But this did not discharge them from their debts, and those of them who had given up their jobs to pursue the will-o'-the-wisp found that there is no legal obligation to give a sucker an even break. Granada found one unfortunate engineering fitter who had borrowed £3,600, and with the interest set at more than 20 per cent his repayments amounted to considerably more than his monthly earnings. He was by no means the only, or the worst affected case.

The lucky ones, relatively speaking, were those who sank their life savings into the operation rather than their jobs and houses. The most grotesque victims were those who persuaded their landladies and landlords to offer their houses as security and then inflicted suffering on both parties. An almost predictable crop of nervous breakdowns, separations and moonlight flits followed. One woman who had been abandoned by her husband after getting into a hopeless well of debt exclaimed, 'It's always been Julian Hodge standing there like three—him, myself and Julian Hodge—always the three of us.' And, of course, there were endless allegations that the 'middle men' between Hodge and Holiday Magic had forged signatures and that details of income had been falsified. The solicitors for the aggrieved parties said they would like to know what sort of commission was being offered to the agents concerned.

In its own defence, the Hodge Group explained that it never knowingly lent money for pyramid selling and that the agents who arranged the loans were independent free-lances responsible only to themselves. This is true. But the MP for a part of Birmingham much affected by the deals—Brian Walden—said that he did not find this satisfactory. 'In my view', he said, 'the bank is responsible for the actions of its own agents, and I do not accept that this business was not drummed up by the agents of the bank.' He went on, in answer to the point that the bank had claimed to check creditworthiness in every case: 'It can't be so. Any proper check would have revealed that many of the people who were raising money in this way were either unemployed or had jobs that did not pay them significant sums of money . . . so that quite frankly I disbelieve the claim that any careful check was done at all.' On the vexed issue of the bank's relationship with the free-lance agents, and the stated intention of the customers themselves, Walden said: 'I would find no difficulty in believing the Hodge explanation if, let's say, forty thousand pounds were involved. But millions were involved. That they didn't know how the business was being got, that they were misled by agents in the field, perhaps so, perhaps so. But it doesn't seem to me to be likely.' He concluded: 'I have a whole series of constituents who will say they received the loan involved in twenty-four hours—an unbelievably short period of time. If any vetting and checking went on, it must have been the quickest operation in the history of banking.'

After Granada had elicited a statement from the Hodge Group denying responsibility for any of the facts unearthed Hodge invited a group of the tenants involved to Cardiff to discuss the issues that were raised by the investigation. But the invitation was conditional on what the Hodge Group called the abandonment of 'fruitless publicity'. The luckless tenants therefore declined the invitations, since nothing had been done for them or even said about them until there was publicity.

The Holiday Magic saga is worth retailing not because there is any stench of illegality about it, nor even because of its 'human

interest'. The point is not to give currency to rumour or speculation. Rather, it is to ask the question, 'Why should a leading
Labour politician, representing a poor and vulnerable electorate
not unlike the wretched working-class families in Birmingham
who went in for pyramid selling, choose Sir Julian Hodge as a
special associate, and take a shareholding in his fringe bank?' For,
although credited as a long-time Labour supporter by friends and
defenders of Callaghan, Hodge's business enterprises have always
been politically impartial. Apart from Callaghan, George Thomas
and at least six other Welsh Labour MPs as shareholders, Hodge
has at various times retained the services of Lord Harlech, a Tory
appointment to the Washington Embassy; Alun Talfan Davies,
a leading Liberal QC; Thomas Merrells, a former Tory Lord
Mayor; Sir Julian Pode, now deceased but an important former
Tory steelmaster, and many others.

In addition to identifying himself with this *galère*, Callaghan has
laid himself open to accusations of being in good standing with
'The Taffia'—a part mythical, part solidly based nexus of individuals who appear to the voters not only to dominate local councils
(where police investigations proceed as we write), but also to
have links with Harlech Television and most of the political
party machines with the notable exception of the Welsh Nationalists. Politics is in some disgrace in South Wales at present, and
Callaghan is one of the many causes of cynicism, not because of
any malpractice, but because of his choice of friends.

So the question resolves itself in a different, political way. Why
should Callaghan risk making himself a public-bar joke in his
beloved constituency? Why should he go out on a limb (and get
sawn off) at the Labour Party Conference in 1971, of all arenas the
one where he is most on familiar ground? Since the Hodge operation is essentially an all-party one, there need be no special
reverberation on the Labour Party. But when the Prime Minister
is himself a subject for gossip, and makes a special virtue of his
concern for 'ordinary folk', it is a cut made against the grain for
him to have associated with the Commercial Bank of Wales.

Although the *Daily Mail* reported Callaghan as saying that 'not
a word of it is true' when some information about his links with
Hodge was published, mainly in *Private Eye*, during his bid for
the leadership, no specific denial has ever appeared and no legal

proceedings instituted. (Callaghan's office at Number Ten maintained this attitude towards the authors of this book. We were warned, 'Don't believe everything you read in *Private Eye*'—but no specific rebuttal of *Private Eye*'s facts was offered.)

The 'constituency man' image does have a respectable background. On several occasions during the first two Wilson administrations Callaghan did take important telephone calls, some of them international ones, in his local pub. He is good at recalling names and faces, and has a fair record of attendance at local party functions and meetings. His agent Jack Brooks says, 'Jim is a delegate from his branch [ward] to the General Management Committee of the constituency party and I think that's very rare with a Member of Parliament', adding the remarkable claim that he has only missed four GMC meetings in thirteen years.

However, in some of the more deprived areas of the constituency, notably Adamstown and Splott, satirical slogans have started appearing, of which 'Jim loves Julian more than Splott' is the most easily printable. This and other disagreements prompted a move to dislodge him from his seat in August 1975. Partly inspired by the then apparently successful attempt to rid Newham North-east of Reginald Prentice, a group of activists in Cardiff South-east led by party vice-chairman Andrew Price signed a letter supporting the Newham rebels and later expressed 'no confidence' in Mr Callaghan, who let it be known that if he was unseated he would resign from the Government and fight the issue through to a conclusion. Faced with such a sledge-hammer response, the local party passed a compromise resolution denying any plot against the sitting member and expressing 'confidence' in him. The vote was not unanimous. One of Mr Price's criticisms had always been of the association between Mr Callaghan and Sir Julian. The member for Cardiff South-east thus enjoys the peculiar distinction of being the only Prime Minister to have fought off a recent constituency revolt partly fuelled by a feeling that it was not his job to associate with a classic capitalist financier.

Two recollections summarise the ambiguity of Callaghan's status as a Welsh, popular figure. One concerns the 1966 election campaign during which fell Callaghan's birthday. He told his supporters and canvassers, many of whom had come from other constituencies because of the excess enthusiasm for Labour that year, that there would be a grand joint celebration of the two happy events. When victory came, the foot-sloggers gathered in the local General and Municipal Workers Union hall for the promised birthday-cum-election jollifications. One of them, leader of a canvassing team and now a Labour MP elsewhere in Wales, recalls: 'He turned up with one bottle of champagne. After a minute or two, I got up and poured my glass back into his. The others did the same, one by one, and we went off to the pub and celebrated properly.'

The second recollection concerns an episode in 1965, when Callaghan was Chancellor of the Exchequer. During the course of a debate on the Finance Bill, when the Labour Government and its narrow majority were under pressure from the Conservative opposition, he observed: 'I do not think of them as the honourable member for X or Y or Z. I look at them and say "investment trusts", "capital speculators" or "that is the fellow who is the Stock Exchange man who makes a profit on gilt edge".' The Tories were furious at his imputations and complained to the Commons Committee on Privileges, which censured Callaghan but took no further action.

It is, then, somewhat ironic that the man who thrives on the image of the common people's affections, and who once denounced the existence of private affluence in the House, should in opposition have gained a harsh reputation among a segment of the non-political and the sarcastic as the owner of a 138-acre farm and the Member of Parliament for the Commercial Bank of Wales.

13

1974–6
Foreign Secretary

'A minister for foreign affairs must be endowed with a sort of instinct which gives him such quick warning that it prevents him from compromising himself in any discussion.'

—CHARLES-MAURICE TALLEYRAND

So far as the public were concerned, the opinion polls got it wrong: they had predicted a Conservative victory in the February 1974 General Election—but in the event Labour won more seats. In fact the polls were not all that inaccurate, for the Conservatives *did* win more votes than Labour. But when these were translated into seats in the new House of Commons, the result was: Labour 301, Conservatives 296, Liberals 14, others (chiefly Scottish and Welsh nationalists and Ulster MPs) 23. (The Speaker brought the total up to 635, the number of constituencies in the Commons following boundary redistribution.) Neither Heath nor Wilson, then, came even close to securing the 318 seats needed for an overall majority.

For four days following the election Heath, still Prime Minister, wrestled with the figures. He invited Jeremy Thorpe, the leader of a temporarily revived Liberal Party, to Downing Street and offered him a place in the Cabinet if the Liberals would join a coalition. In the end Thorpe declined, not least because a combined Conservative–Liberal Government would still be in a minority in the Commons, commanding 310 votes while all other parties voting together could have mustered 324.

Finally the logic of Heath's arithmetic vanquished the fantasies of his dreams: on Monday, 4 March he resigned as Prime Minister, and the Queen invited Wilson to form a minority Government. With little delay he appointed Callaghan Foreign Secretary.

It was just what Callaghan wanted. While in opposition he had made good use of the portfolio, especially as it gave him title to speak on the European issue. This had the double bonus of reconciling statesmanship with party popularity. Once installed in the Foreign Office, however, and with the main exception of the EEC (see Chapter 14) he found this balance a harder one to strike. In a Fabian pamphlet *Challenges and Opportunities for British Foreign Policy*, which he published in December 1975 under the name of Jim Callaghan, he wrote: 'Foreign policy is not an idol to be hidden in the temple, untouched by profane hands . . . it should not and cannot be left as the sole prerogative of a few foreign policy "experts".'

Callaghan did not, however, seem to apply this philosophy to the Labour Party itself. Only one month before, the party's NEC had been circulated with an acrimonious memo by Ian Mikardo on the Foreign Secretary's attitude towards the membership. After making a series of points about Cyprus, Chile, Indonesia and Brazil, Mikardo ended by complaining of Callaghan's non-attendance at meetings of the International Committee: 'When he was asked why not he said "it's not because I'm too busy, it's that I've no desire to attend a committee which has people on it like Frank Allaun and Joan Maynard and Alex Kitson".'

Whatever may be thought about these three stalwarts of the left (and Anthony Crosland, now Foreign Secretary, is fond of saying that it's always the left who are obsessed with foreign affairs) it means that certain profane hands, and not only the three mentioned above, were kept off the idol. NEC members recall for instance that in April 1974 Callaghan lost his temper when Michael Foot appealed to him to halt arms shipments to Chile.

Indeed, instead of involving the Labour Party in foreign-policy making, Callaghan sought his inspiration elsewhere. In large measure, his own stature rose and fell in time with that of Dr Henry Kissinger, whose relationship with Callaghan was, throughout, close both personally and politically. Callaghan even rang him up to commiserate at particularly awkward moments of the Nixon resignation saga; and Kissinger agreed to join in the celebrations which attended Callaghan's receipt of the freedom of Cardiff.

In a sense, Kissinger's crises were Callaghan's crises. And

nowhere more so than in one of the few remaining areas where substantial British and American interests overlap—the Eastern Mediterranean.

Bitter Lessons: The Partition of Cyprus

On 15 July 1974 the ruling military junta in Athens used its control over the Cyprus National Guard to overthrow the government of Archbishop Makarios. Thus began the first phase of a three-act tragedy. Heavy fighting ensued, though it was chiefly confined to rival Greek political factions on the island. Turkish citizens were not at this stage threatened, but nonetheless the Turkish Government warned that it regarded the action of Athens as controverting the 1960 Treaty which guaranteed Cyprus's independence, and threatened to take action herself. Bulent Ecevit, then Prime Minister of Turkey, travelled to London and suggested that the British might join him in a peace-keeping operation as joint guarantors of the Treaty. Callaghan, for reasons which remain unclear and disputed, declined the offer. This led to the second act. The Turks made a preliminary landing on the island on 20 July, which precipitated the collapse of the five-day-old pro-*enosis* junta headed by Nicos Sampson. The parent dictatorship in Athens also expired as a result. A preliminary ceasefire followed on 22 July, leading to the first Geneva Conference. Further talks at Geneva, chaired by James Callaghan, broke down on 14 August, bringing about the third act—a massive four-day onslaught by Turkey which left her in control of 40 per cent of the island. This portion she still retains, having made one-third of the Greek Cypriots refugees and inflicted heavy damage and casualties. Taken together, the three stages of this crisis presented Callaghan with the severest test of his Foreign Secretaryship.

Callaghan had first grappled with the intricacies of Cyprus while Kissinger was still at Harvard. As a front-bench spokesman in July 1960 he had launched a furious attack on the record of the Macmillan Government, citing Eden's *Memoirs* as proof of a divide-and-rule strategy. Callaghan mocked the Conservatives for granting independence only six years after they proclaimed Britain's 'indefinite sovereignty' over the island. The 600 lives and the millions of pounds lost in communal fighting, he suggested, were a waste. But after Makarios and his supporters achieved the independence of the island, Callaghan does not seem to have shown any continuing interest: from 1964 to 1970 he was in government himself, with departmental interests elsewhere.

Britain's responsibilities in Cyprus survived independence. In 1960 the Cypriots conceded Britain 90 square miles of their territory for sovereign base areas, in the expectation that a measure of British protection would be available in an emergency. Furthermore, under a treaty also signed in 1960, Britain was a joint guarantor, with Greece and Turkey, of Cypriot independence. The United Nations mediator, in his 1965 report, wrote of the British bases as representing 'to a certain degree, an additional military guarantee of the integrity of Cyprus'.

The United States, however, had other ideas. American policy in the region had long been that Cypriot independence was expendable if it weakened NATO. One plan, promulgated by Dean Acheson, Cyprus mediator for President Johnson, as long ago as 1964, had been to unify the island with Greece, but to provide a Turkish canton in the north with a military base. Other less subtle schemes were also put forward, but all amounted to *de facto* partition of the island. Archbishop Makarios's persistent refusal to consider any of these plans gained him the reputation among Washington officials as 'the cassocked Castro': 'God damn it, Your Beatitude', George Ball, Under-Secretary of State, once exclaimed to him during a particularly difficult interview.

This mild tension developed ugly undertones after the Greek armed forces seized power in Athens in 1967. They began, with American foreknowledge if not with actual connivance, to 'destabilize' the Cypriot Government. A recent report on covert intelligence, from a Congressional Committee chaired by Congressman Otis Pike, concluded that the Central Intelligence Agency possessed the material necessary to forecast the first act of the 1974 tragedy—the coup which toppled Makarios (but failed to kill him) and installed Nicos Sampson. And there is considerable evidence, unearthed by American journalists such as Laurence Stern of the *Washington Post*, to suggest not only that the CIA actually *did* know of the Sampson coup, but that the coup was facilitated by the close security and defence connections between Washington and the Athens junta.

In addition to what American intelligence knew, Archbishop Makarios issued a direct warning that a coup against his Government was imminent—just two weeks before the first shot was fired. Yet, in the early stages of the crisis, when time was of paramount importance, the British Government did nothing. In the view of Lord Caradon, Governor of Cyprus in the 1950s and British representative to the United Nations in the 1960s, 'All the evil subsequently flowed from that decision, taken under United States influence, to let it run. Everything else piled up like a traffic accident in fog.'

Throughout the 1974 crisis the United States strongly discouraged Britain from taking an independent initiative—and Foreign Office officials recalling the Suez débâcle in 1956 knew precisely how crippling the lack of American support can be. But America's posture did not disturb Callaghan: he was content to leave the problem to the Americans, and admitted privately that no British policy on Cyprus could run counter to Dr Kissinger's.

Callaghan only felt misgivings on one occasion that can be verified. At Kissinger's request he chaired the Geneva Conference which followed the initial Turkish landings, as Kissinger had to return to Washington for the final days of the Watergate scandal, culminating in President Nixon's resignation on 10 August. This left Callaghan in his favourite role of 'honest broker'. During the talks, however, he discovered that Kissinger and his staff had been negotiating with the Turks behind the backs of the British delegation.

A further revelation came when Callaghan was dining with the chief Greek Cypriot negotiator Glafkos Clerides on the night of 9 August. According to Polyvios Polyviou, legal adviser to the Greek Cypriot delegation, Callaghan was shown captured Turkish documents which clearly presaged a forthcoming Turkish invasion out of their bridgeheads to seize a large part of the island. 'What came through most strongly', says Polyviou, 'was that Callaghan was totally dependent on Kissinger and in constant communication with him in the latter stages. But by these documents he was totally taken aback, as though it was the first time he realized Turkey was not prepared to negotiate.' A member of the British delegation recalls Callaghan's shock at the way his 'honest broker' role was undermined by both the United States and Turkey. Callaghan had evidently underestimated the power of *realpolitik* which persuaded the Americans to switch support from the Greek colonels, whose junta had collapsed when Nicos Sampson failed to sustain his coup, to the newly aggressive and more powerful Turks.

A few hours after the Geneva talks broke down on 14 August, the Turkish army launched the invasion which captured almost half the island.

For a NATO ally—Turkey—to invade a friendly Commonwealth country—Cyprus—would pose great problems for any British Foreign Secretary. Callaghan, however, felt powerless to act, despite the 1960 Treaty and the British troops in the sovereign base area. And whatever misgivings he felt about Kissinger's relations with the Turks, he was still prepared to take his cue from the American Secretary of State. At a NATO foreign ministers' meeting in December 1974, Kissinger said he was under great Congressional pressure to make the Turks concede ground in Cyprus; but in order to have any leverage, he needed something to offer Turkey. Would Callaghan allow the Turkish Cypriot refugees who were sheltering in their thousands in British base areas to travel north, to Turkey, or the part of Cyprus under Turkish control?

Callaghan did what Kissinger asked. He stopped at the Akrotiri base in Cyprus on his way to Africa on 15 January 1975. The Greek side begged him not to hand over the refugees to Turkey. They said that in that event, the Turks would be repatriated to the north of Cyprus, ensconced in former Greek property, and no *quid pro quo* would follow. But Callaghan did not heed the pleas, and the airlift began. Everything turned out as the Greeks had feared. The racial partition of Cyprus began from that moment, and no Turkish reciprocal gesture was made. But Dr Kissinger did gain a few days' grace in his tussle with Congress.

Not long afterwards, the House of Commons set up a Select Committee on Cyprus, which visited the island and began a detailed investigation. Early in 1976, Callaghan tried to strip the committee of its power 'to call for persons and papers', a surprise move, which in any case was defeated in the House. He then declined to appear before it for several weeks: the *Sunday Times* noted on 18 January that 'Mr Callaghan is simply refusing to come before the Select Committee'. Finally, one month later and flanked by three civil servants, he made his appearance. He had, in essence, two choices. One was to admit that the policy had not been a success, and face probing questions. The other was to maintain ignorance and to stonewall questioning. At some cost to his public image he chose the second, and astounded journalists and diplomats present by the things he affected not to know.

Questioned on whether he still recognised the original Treaty of Guarantee: 'I do not know the law as clearly as some.'

On whether he had made preparations with the Ministry of Defence before the Turkish invasion: 'I do not know what you are referring to.'

On anticipating the invasion: 'Nobody knew where the invasion was likely to come from, whether from Greece or Turkey.'

On reports of Turkish troop movements which he had received at the Geneva talks: 'Was that right?' (turning to his aide Mr Goodison).

On whether the British forces in the north of Cyprus could have been deployed in a different way: 'I suppose so. I do not know.'

On whether there were enough British forces to have secured the northern coast: 'I am not able to comment on that because I just do not know at this stage.'

On whether there had been direct discussions between Greek and Turkish Cypriots on bi-zonal federations: 'I do not remember' (Mr Goodison took over).

On whether Archbishop Makarios had accepted the three-point settlement or not: 'I think you are going beyond my knowledge' (Mr Goodison took over).

On whether British citizens had been assured of British Government protection in the event of war, and if he understood the relevant clause in the Treaty: 'I am sorry, where is that . . . I can only repeat this parrot-wise, but I am told this has nothing to do with the Treaty of Guarantee.'

On whether the Turkish Government had changed its mind on compensation: (Mr Burden had to answer for him).

On whether the Foreign Office in 1974 had advised British residents not to return to their homes: 'When was this advice given, could you tell me?' Told that it was October 1974, by the Consular Emergency Unit of the FO: 'What did it say?'

On the status of refugees within British sovereign base areas: 'I doubt if I can answer that. Mr Goodison had better try.'

On whether the High Commissioner had a hardship fund: 'I am afraid I am not aware of that.'

Callaghan's *gaucherie* on this occasion left most observers baffled and surprised. He was asked by a Tory member of the committee whether the Government had any advance intelligence of the 15 July coup. He replied 'No.' 'You mean you cannot say?' 'No, there was no advance intelligence.' Even the fact that Makarios had publicised his own foreknowledge of the coup did not weigh with Callaghan. Nor did all the recent evidence about State Department forecasts cut any ice. Asked about United States involvement he answered that he did not think the Americans knew, or indeed that anyone except the Greek junta and their Cypriot allies knew. Yet Thomas Boyatt, head of the State Department Cyprus desk, is known to have anticipated the putsch, and Henry Tasca, the US Ambassador in Athens, is known to have had public misgivings about the part played by the CIA.

On 19 May 1976, the Select Committee on Cyprus presented its report to Parliament. It complained at the attempts made to obstruct its work, and the unwillingness of Callaghan to reveal any details of his discussions at the time. It remarked that 'If it is true that the three stages of the Cyprus crisis came as a surprise to the British Government, this argues deficiencies in Government intelligence which ought to be remedied.' It noted that the French Government appeared to have known of each move in advance, despite having a far smaller stake in the region. And it concluded: 'Britain had a legal right to intervene, she had a moral obligation to intervene, she had the military capacity to intervene. She did not intervene for reasons which the Government refuses to give.' Only by the casting vote of the chairman, Arthur Bottomley, did the Select Committee not include the sentences: 'The Foreign Secretary's policies are totally negative. His pessimism and lack of ideas or initiatives is profoundly depressing.'

Foreign Office reaction was prompt and angry. It concentrated on the practical difficulties raised by a British intervention; Brigadier Michael Harbottle, a former commander of United Nations forces on the island, however, gave his agreement to the committee's judgement. On the other hand, one junior minister in private complained of the intellectual 'snobbery' with which the committee discussed Callaghan's evasiveness and shortcomings of diction. The case here was somewhat spoilt by repeated references to the large number of Cypriot constituents represented by some of the committee MPs concerned, which was an ethnically snobbish judgement of its own. But the fact remains, very little comfort was offered for Callaghan's own role. The recommendations of the committee may indeed have to be taken with a pinch of salt; the condemnation is not so much that the then Foreign Secretary failed, but that he cannot escape the charge that he did not really try.

In his effort to acquit himself of collusion in the Cyprus tragedy, Callaghan convicted himself of ignorance. He even underestimated the number of refugees by 50 per cent (which wounded Cypriot opinion) and at one point appeared to give implicit recognition to the illegal 'Turkish Federated State', which caused the Foreign Office to issue a hasty press release setting the record straight. It was, altogether, a poor performance. Faced with the first big challenge of his Foreign Secretaryship, and with one of the last historic chances to use British influence outside Europe, Callaghan left the running of policy to Dr Kissinger—with disastrous results. If, as his Fabian pamphlet says, foreign policy should not be kept as a sacred 'idol untouched by profane hands' it is ironic that on this occasion he handed it over to the greatest high priest of them all.

The Hare and the Fox: Britain's War with Iceland

Aphorism has it that nine times out of ten the hare will manage to escape the fox. This is because while the fox is running for his lunch, the hare is running for his life. During Callaghan's term at the Foreign Office Britain's third 'cod war' with Iceland broke out—precipitated by the expiry of the temporary agreement between London and Reykjavik made after the Heath Government had lost the previous war (as an earlier Conservative administration had lost the first). It was always inevitable that the Icelanders would manage the hat-trick. Iceland receives 81 per cent of her foreign exchange and export earnings from fish. The United Kingdom receives only 0·2 per cent of hers from the same source. Every Icelander knows these figures, every Icelandic political party and newspaper is obsessed with them. Very few British voters are directly involved. The fox and hare analogy could hardly be better illustrated.

Throughout the dispute, an international conference on the law of the sea was pending. This, it was universally assumed, would legitimise Icelandic claims for a limit of 200 miles, which is rapidly becoming the international custom and practice. The atmosphere of anomaly and irony was completed when the conference took place and the British team committed itself to a 12-mile territorial sea and a 200-mile exclusive zone for all coastal states.

It is hard to think of a more coastal state than Iceland, most of the interior of which is totally barren and uncultivable. As long ago as 1966, Research Paper 10 of the International Council for the Exploration of the Sea found that British trawlers were catching 30·6 per cent of all cod in Icelandic waters by weight, but 52·9 by number of cod landed. Roughly translated, many of the cod were too small, too young and had had no chance to breed. In the late sixties, Iceland saw her entire herring stock 'fished out', with traumatic results for employment and productivity which are by no means forgotten today. This history made for Icelandic intransigence from the very beginning, and it is difficult to see how any British Government—especially with the recent experience of watching a Tory Government have to climb down under identical conditions—could possibly imagine that it could improve on the Conservatives' uninspiring record.

Yet under Callaghan, Labour forcibly resisted the Icelandic claim because it had been made 'unilaterally'. The position became even more absurd and complicated when President Ford, every bit as 'unilaterally', signed an Act of Congress which exactly followed Iceland's example. Long before, the West Germans had made their own pact with Iceland, and NATO was putting pressure on Britain to settle with Iceland before the Icelanders withdrew from the alliance in protest, as they had many times threatened to do. The runic writing was clearly on the wall from the start. Yet frigates and trawlers engaged in a grotesque North Atlantic ballet, there were several collisions and it was a miracle that no lives were lost.

To a certain extent, the Foreign Office was circumscribed by decisions taken and attitudes struck elsewhere in Whitehall. The undistinguished Fred Peart, Minister for Agriculture, Fisheries and Food, and Wilson as Prime Minister were in favour of out-facing the Icelanders. But the final responsibility rested with the Foreign Office, and with a Foreign Secretary who denounced Icelandic claims as 'unreasonable in themselves' (House of Commons, 4 February 1976) as well as unilateral, while at the same time advancing the same set of claims for Britain on the international scene.

In part, the blame must rest with the Prime Minister and the Minister of Agriculture and Fisheries, both of whom behaved throughout as spokesmen for the industry. Yet as late as February 1976 Callaghan told the House of Commons that 'as our fleet is in international waters, if they are interfered with then the Navy will protect them. That is the simple position. I wish to go no further.' 'There are times', says one of Callaghan's former tutors at Nuffield College, Oxford, 'when a little ectoplasmic John Bull manifests itself over his shoulder.' This was one of them. Perhaps Callaghan was subconsciously recalling his time with Naval Intelligence in Iceland during the war—only then Britain had pre-emptively occupied the island.

In early May 1976, at a meeting of the Overseas Policy and Defence Group of the Cabinet, an alliance of Roy Hattersley, Michael Foot, Roy Jenkins and Roy Mason was enough to overcome the entrenched support for the fisheries lobby from the Minister of Agriculture and his supporters such as Lord Elwyn-Jones. 'The amazing thing', said one of the participants, 'is not that we've beaten Ag and Fish at last, but that they managed to lead us up the garden path for so long.' The meeting remained convinced that British claims were just, but was now converted to the view that right did not mean might. This contradiction having once been faced and accepted, the road to a climb-down was open, even if it did embarrass the new Foreign Secretary, Anthony Crosland, who represented the sturdy fishing constituency of

Grimsby. On 2 June, British frigates were withdrawn from the disputed fishing grounds, and sufficient concessions were offered to the Icelanders to melt their intransigence about their only resource. It was agreed at a meeting in Oslo between Mr Crosland and his Icelandic counterpart Mr Agustsson, that the number of British trawlers in the zone should be kept to twenty-four at any one time, pending the next Law of the Sea conference which was expected to ratify the 200-mile norm and open the way to a general agreement between Iceland and the EEC.

In the general relief, nobody made much of the fact that the 60,000-ton cod quota for Britain was a little less than the previous Icelandic offer, made in November and rejected out of hand by the Foreign Office during Callaghan's term. At his appearance before the Select Committee on Cyprus, Mr Callaghan had quoted Bismarck to the effect that large countries were more responsible than smaller ones because they had more to be responsible about. As the seven-month fiasco of war with Iceland fizzled out, Mr Callaghan, as in so many cases, was no longer there.

Callaghan and Africa

When Joan Lestor became his Minister of State at the Foreign Office in March 1974, Callaghan told a group of civil servants, 'Miss Lestor's to be our conscience in this department. And we all know what we do with our consciences, don't we?' A year later he had her transferred to the Ministry of Education. Displeased by the move, she marched in and asked him for the reason. Not in the least put out by her directness, Callaghan replied, 'You see, my dear, the trouble is that I like to have people around me who are *friends* of mine.' As she now says, 'Jim is a very kind man and very pleasant to work with—until you cross him.'

The main source of their dispute was the vexed question of Africa—an issue which was also. causing widespread disquiet throughout the Labour Party. Almost as soon as Labour took office a fierce row erupted in the party over a British naval exercise and visit to Simonstown; Benn, Lestor and others in the Government voted at the NEC for a motion attacking the Cabinet. Callaghan was furious. He several times said, 'You can't afford to get too far ahead of public opinion on these things'—a familiar echo of his attitude to politics.

In fact, British policy had been running in very much the same groove on Southern Africa throughout the ten years since Rhodesia declared unilateral independence. A bi-partisan commitment to majority rule existed, and was adhered to in varying degrees of enthusiasm whichever party was in power. Traditionally speaking, Labour had always had better contacts with the leaders of black independent states to the north, many of whom had built up a relationship with the party, and with Callaghan personally, during the struggle against the Conservatives for decolonisation.

On Southern Africa, Callaghan managed to get two things working in tandem—his personal powers of persuasion and his relationship with Dr Kissinger. The latter, on this occasion, was not the one-way street it had been over Cyprus, and though at the time of writing the future is uncertain, Callaghan has already demonstrated his ability to give advice as well as take it. Angola, too, has proved a powerfully persuasive answer both to those who wished to engage Britain on the losing side in Africa, and to those who wished to continue the 'do-nothing' policy followed so colourfully and so long by Wilson.

Callaghan had, in fact, been in favour of military intervention in Rhodesia at certain points in the Wilson–Smith duet during the sixties. The settler revolt had antagonised him considerably, and he felt that Britain could do better than be flouted by such a mediocre gang. But he was overruled in Cabinet, and in any case had many other things with which to preoccupy himself.

In 1969 the National Security Council of the USA was directed by Kissinger, on the instructions of President Nixon, to prepare 'a comprehensive review of US policy toward Southern Africa'. Its conclusions were highly cynical and redolent of spurious *realpolitik*. In particular, it totally underestimated the fragility of the Portuguese empire. Of the British stance in the region it said: 'The UK has historically been heavily involved throughout the region . . . perhaps the overriding UK interest is the importance for her balance of payments of trade, earnings on investment, and other invisibles from South Africa. Investment alone in that country is estimated at $3,000m. This key interest explains UK reluctance to move decisively on a range of southern African issues, such as South-West Africa where it abstained on the key

UN General Assembly resolution which determined that South Africa had forfeited its mandate, or even on Southern Rhodesia where the UK has indicated it will not support the extension of mandatory sanctions.' The memorandum sustained this tone of voice throughout, but the collapse of Portugal's 'civilising mission' in 1974, and the subsequent sweep to power of the Russian-backed MPLA (People's Movement for the Liberation of Angola) against forces backed and funded by the United States and South Africa, rather altered the picture.

Faced with these events, Americans began to re-think their policies. Senator Dick Clark, chairman of the Africa sub-committee of the Foreign Relations Committee in Washington, led the fight to block funds for Kissinger's adventure in Angola, and announced subsequently that 'we've backed the has-beens rather than the will-be's'. In the first week of May 1976, Henry Kissinger appeared in Lusaka and warned the Smith regime that it could expect no support from the United States if it persisted in denying majority rule. He also offered financial help to any African nation that made sacrifices in the coming struggle, and even extended the olive branch to the government of Angola if it would dispense with the thousands of Cuban troops within its borders. Although attacked by Smith, who denounced him for not visiting Rhodesia on his tour, Kissinger earned guarded praise from many African leaders, particularly ones considered 'responsible', such as Kenneth Kaunda.

Experience in this case had evidently been a great teacher, but so had James Callaghan. In June 1975, at the CENTO (Central European Treaty Organisation) meeting in Ankara, Callaghan had argued with Kissinger that a 'de-stabilization' policy for Portugal would be disastrous. Specifically, he had pointed out that it would make life unbearable for the one group who commanded popular support, and would remain loyal to the west—the Portuguese Socialist Party, whose leader Mario Soares was an old acquaintance of Callaghan. Not without misgivings, Kissinger had accepted this advice. Now in Africa he had learned that Manichaean anti-Communism and anti-revolutionary policies were indeed a blind alley. The thing was to get on the right side of the 'will-be's'.

*

Southern Africa and its white dominions are currently fringed by four independent states, none of them strong economically or stable politically. 'The four Presidents'—Samora Machel of Mozambique, Julius Nyerere of Tanzania, Kenneth Kaunda of Zambia (where Kissinger made his speech) and Seretse Khama of Botswana, are the key to political developments. One of Callaghan's junior ministers recalls that 'until he visited KK in Lusaka, Jim didn't know how great the Zambian sacrifice had been in maintaining sanctions'. There were, indeed, a number of things that Callaghan had not appreciated sufficiently until his visit. But his tour of Africa was perhaps the outstanding performance of his Foreign Secretaryship.

In December 1974–January 1975 Callaghan flew 25,000 miles and visited seven black African capitals, making the fullest use of his former standing as Labour's opposition spokesman on colonial policy. With Kenneth Kaunda, for instance, he was able to recall that the last letter he sent to him had arrived the day before his arrest by colonial police. Similar memories lightened his meeting with Jomo Kenyatta. The seven-nation safari revived much of the goodwill, which had lapsed under the Conservatives, between London and the black Commonwealth. It also gave additional leverage to the efforts of President Nyerere, whose influence with the African guerrilla fighters in Rhodesia itself was activated. The hope was that by clamping down on ceasefire violations and securing the release of detainees in Salisbury, the intransigent settler group around Ian Smith could be persuaded to concede, or at least isolated if they did not.

In pursuit of this, and foreshadowing the strategy to come, Callaghan also visited South Africa during his tour and conferred with John Vorster, the South African Prime Minister, in Port Elizabeth. He told him that Britain did not recognise the right of South African police to operate on the Rhodesian border, and urged him to withdraw them. Although Callaghan was widely denounced in the Nationalist and Afrikaaner press of the Republic, it seemed that Mr Vorster was still not deflected from his policy of détente with the surrounding African states. At Victoria Falls in the autumn of 1975, Vorster and Dr Kaunda met without any ostensible British presence at all, however. A lone High

Commissioner was stationed in a hotel some miles from the actual meeting, and H.M.'s Government preferred to keep a low profile.

This delicate diplomacy was not given time to succeed. The bitter civil war in Angola, which saw Vorster heavily criticised by his own extremists, made swift changes of policy both necessary and possible. Even as the American strategy in Angola was falling apart, Mr Callaghan despatched Sir Antony Duff to South Africa and Lord Greenhill to Rhodesia. The details of their respective February meetings—neither was empowered to do any negotiating —were both swiftly imparted to Kissinger. Sir Antony, in fact, left for Washington from South Africa itself. The fact that he had done so was not revealed until afterwards, which gave rise to suspicion in some quarters that there was a deal being done behind closed doors.

In reality a new turn of strategy was being proposed. In a statement to the House of Commons on 22 March 1976, Callaghan reiterated warnings of war and announced no retreat on majority rule conditions (and also gave himself a statesmanlike image for the Labour leadership contest). His policy involved giving two ambitious hostages to fortune. The first of these was and is a gamble—that South Africa would be persuaded to ditch the Rhodesian Front and that Ian Smith's trump card as 'an outpost of the West' would be stolen from him. The second, cutting with the grain of increased white settler nervousness in general, was the offer of funds for repatriation and reconstruction if they would concede the principle of early majority rule. There are, under Callaghan's own original definition of the word, almost 160,000 'patrials' in Rhodesia, and although it is extremely difficult to be certain, something in the region of one million Britons who can claim Rhodesian relatives.

Callaghan is too experienced not to worry that a racial war in Southern Africa could destroy the delicate bi-partisan view of Rhodesia in British politics. The strategy has been, then, to put as much pressure as possible on Ian Smith without causing domestic repercussions and a possible sharp rise in racial tensions. By the time that Henry Kissinger made his Lusaka speech, in May 1976, Callaghan had secured approval of his 22 March statement from 'the Four Presidents', from the EEC countries and from the State Department. It was rejected with scorn by

Salisbury but not, crucially, by Pretoria. It was in its way a considerable achievement, and done with such skill and diplomacy that few people in the Labour Party realised that their Government was now effectively allied with the execrated regime of *apartheid*. There was a brief flare-up when the government ministers on the NEC rejected a proposal in May 1976 to wage trade war against South Africa; but the issue was not pressed to a serious confrontation by the left. Nor has the illegal South African occupation of South-West Africa (Namibia) been allowed to obstruct negotiations. Indeed, the British-based corporation Rio Tinto Zinc has secured a contract to mine uranium there. Once again the onus of concessions has been laid on Pretoria.

In Africa, Callaghan shone, at least by comparison. He talked Henry Kissinger out of a stance of cold-war brinkmanship. He healed the inherited antagonism between Wilson and Kaunda. He rescued Mr Denis Hills from the firing squads of General Amin by a lightning personal visit to Kampala in June 1975. He maintained the pressure on Ian Smith while opening the door to possible white dissenters. But, at the end of the diplomatic saga, he and Dr Kissinger had staked everything on the South Africans seeing sense. If the gamble fails, the judgement will be a harsh one, and it will illustrate the perennial differences between Callaghan's short-term skill and long-term capacity.

14

1974-6
Common Market
Odyssey

'The only really materialistic people I have ever met have been the Europeans.'

—MARY MCCARTHY

Enoch Powell voted Labour in February 1974 for one reason: he wanted Britain to leave the Common Market, and the only chance of this coming about lay with Labour's promise to re-negotiate the terms of entry, and to put the results to the test of a special General Election or 'consultative referendum'. Powell's opposition to the EEC derived not from the threat to food prices, or the lack of fairness in the Community's budgetary arrangements; he based his arguments on the more fundamental issue of the sovereignty of the British Parliament.

Had the February General Election produced a decisive victor, Powell's intervention would not have mattered. But as Labour returned to power without an overall Commons majority, and with a lead of only five seats over the Conservatives, anything which swayed enough voters to give Labour three or four extra seats can be said to have 'won' the election for the party. Although there can never be final, undisputed proof, it seems likely that the 'Powell effect' was sufficiently strong to give Wilson rather than Heath the opportunity to form a minority Government. If this is so, then there is little doubt that a short passage in Labour's February manifesto must count among the electorally most valuable words ever written:

'If re-negotiations are successful, it is the policy of the Labour Party that, in view of the unique importance of the decision, the people should have the right to decide the issue through a General Election or Consultative Referendum ... If re-negotiations do not succeed, we shall not regard the Treaty obligations as binding on us. We shall then put to the British people the reasons why we find the new terms unacceptable, and consult them on the advisability of negotiating our withdrawal from the Communities.'

To all appearances this pledge was a victory for the anti-marketeers in the Labour Party. But Wilson and Callaghan had a more sophisticated reason for embracing the principle of a referendum. (Formally, the decision to hold a referendum rather than a special General Election was not taken until re-negotiations were almost complete; in practice, a referendum was always the more likely choice.) As we have seen, Callaghan believed as early as 1972 that once Britain joined the EEC, she might well have to stay a member, for the problems of withdrawal would be vastly greater then the penalties of continued membership. Equally, Callaghan knew that for a Labour Government to say so openly and clearly would be to risk a profound split inside the party. With some skill and a little luck, a successful referendum would solve the problem, for while the Labour Party could always campaign against what a Labour Government decided, it would be silenced by a decisive 'Yes' vote from the people.

It is therefore stretching political calculation only slightly to say that the promise of a referendum not only put Labour into power by offering—to Enoch Powell, at least—the chance of Britain pulling *out* of the EEC; it also gave Wilson and Callaghan the opportunity of maintaining party unity in government by offering a device which would enable Labour to keep Britain *in* the EEC.

This does not mean that the re-negotiations Callaghan conducted between June 1974 and March 1975 were meaningless. Rather, it means that Callaghan's actions must be measured against his domestic political objective.

A trade union negotiator would, perhaps, best recognise Callaghan's re-negotiation style—rejection of the first offer, followed by drawn-out talks over the points of disagreement, then hard bargaining on details, ending up with the reluctant endorsement of 'the best agreement we could get'.

Callaghan's 'rejection' phase was as short as political decency allowed. He told the EEC Council of Ministers in Luxembourg on 1 April 1974 that the Government opposed continued membership on the terms which the Conservatives had negotiated. He went on to make his demands, reading from the Labour manifesto: 'major changes in the Common Agricultural Policy... fairer methods of financing the Community budget... we would reject economic and monetary union... no harmonisation of value added tax... retention by Parliament of powers to pursue effective regional, industrial and fiscal policies... the economic interests of the Commonwealth and the developing countries must be safeguarded.' Callaghan said he would 'prefer' the re-negotiations to be successful: 'To some extent that will depend upon us—but it will also depend upon the attitude of the other partners in the negotiations.'

The other EEC foreign ministers were shocked by what they heard. Michel Jobert of France said there could be no re-negotiations of treaty obligations: 'We agreed to pay a fair price for Britain's entry. We do not see the need to pay a supplementary price to keep her in.' Renaat Van Elslande of Belgium confessed that he could not 'digest' the concept of re-negotiation. Only the Germans failed to join in public expressions of disapproval.

The real point of the Luxembourg speech, however, was made in the following weekend in the *Sunday Times* by Nicholas Carroll, a journalist with a close knowledge of how Britain's Foreign Office behaves: 'The abrasive entry into Europe last week of James Callaghan was far from the blundering, bull-in-a-china-shop performance widely reported at the time... Behind it lay a calculated Cabinet strategy, deliberately designed to shock his European colleagues into action... It is claimed that in private talks in Luxembourg the other foreign ministers were much less cold than their formal statements indicated; the Government is particularly pleased with Chancellor Willy Brandt's subsequent understanding of the Labour Party's political problems. The main point is that while it would have been possible for Mr Callaghan to have employed a more gentlemanly approach to the council, he could not have carried Britain's Cabinet or the country if he had done so. Reports from the party's grassroots are apparently very encouraging: there is said to be widespread delight over the way Mr Callaghan handled the whole thing.'

F

*

During the following eight weeks a 'sea change'—in the words of one close colleague—took place in Callaghan's attitude. He revelled in a weekend meeting of the foreign ministers of the nine EEC countries at Schloss Gymnich near Bonn on 20–21 April, finding considerable attractions in the idea of formulating a joint foreign policy. As the meeting ended he even embraced Jobert, his critic of 1 April, and said: 'Thank you for helping me through this first meeting.' Another foreign minister, knowing how to get through to Callaghan, told him: 'You don't think Dr Kissinger would stop off in London on his way to Moscow if Britain were not part of the Common Market, do you?' The point struck home; Callaghan began to see Britain's membership not just as a matter of political tactics, but as desirable in itself. He became, for all practical purposes, a Common Market convert.

Towards the end of May Callaghan persuaded the Cabinet to make what was possibly its most important single decision concerning the re-negotiations: he could return to Luxembourg and tell the other EEC countries that the changes Britain wanted did *not* involve any changes to the Treaty of Rome, or any of the other basic legal ties which bind member states. Ever since, Britain's pro-Market ministers have reflected with amazement how easily the point was won. 'If Benn or Foot or Peter Shore had fought us on this,' according to one pro-Marketeer, 'they could well have made re-negotiation impossible. Altering the treaties was the one thing we knew the other countries would never accept.'

When Callaghan next spoke in Luxembourg on 4 June, he was certainly more conciliatory: 'In our judgement Ministers will find that the proposals I shall put before you, if accepted, would not require changes in the treaties.' In contrast to his April speech, Callaghan made no threat of withdrawal; instead he looked forward to 'an early and successful result for these re-negotiations . . . If they secure the approval of the British people we shall be ready to play our full part in constructing a new Europe . . . Let us together put these matters right and when we do then the Community will be once again strengthened to play a constructive part in the affairs of Europe and in bringing its influence to bear on the problems of the world.'

Callaghan intended this speech to have a political Doppler effect—so that it would sound differently, depending on where the listener was standing. The next day *The Times* reported the response of the other EEC countries: 'Britain's partners were greatly relieved at Mr Callaghan's change of tone since his harsh and threatening initial statement on 1 April. They were not prepared to concede straight away that Britain had a genuine grievance over the entry terms negotiated by the Conservatives. But his desire to carry on all "re-negotiations" within the existing Community machinery of Commission and Council without revising treaties was particularly welcomed.' The Council of Ministers agreed to ask the European Commission—the Common Market's civil service, in effect—to draw up 'a detailed inventory of economic and financial developments within the Community since its enlargement, with projections for the future'. In other words, re-negotiation would now be accepted; what they all wanted was an agenda.

Callaghan's speech achieved exactly the right effect on his Common Market audience. He was equally concerned, however, that his British, especially Labour Party, audience would hear something slightly different: his determination to fight for better membership terms. For, however convinced Callaghan was in his own mind that Britain would have to stay a member of the EEC, it was important to be *seen* as a tough, still sceptical negotiator. But the anti-Marketeers were already suspicious. During a House of Commons debate on 11 June, Douglas Jay—one of the most fervent critics of Market membership—asked: 'Does Mr Callaghan stand by everything he said in his speech on 1 April?' Callaghan replied: 'Certainly: there is no contradiction between the two speeches except in the minds of the interpreters. I have gone through the contents and I defy anyone to point out where there is any contradiction between the two.' So for home consumption, April's hard line remained a valid text for government policy—an impression Callaghan sought to bolster by coming to the debate having just vetoed a Common Market resolution which called for a commitment to 'European union'.

For the time being, Callaghan was successful. Some anti-Market Labour MPs had come to the Commons debate intending to force a vote criticising Callaghan for deviating from Labours' manifesto conditions for continued membership. Callaghan's speech persuaded them not to.

One reason why Callaghan managed to outmanœuvre anti-Market MPs on this occasion—and, indeed, throughout the re-negotiations—was that he denied them the ground they would really have liked to fight on. For anyone opposed to the EEC in principle, the details of the re-negotiations obscured the central issue. But to argue this case would be to depart from the February manifesto, which judged British membership on the *terms*, not the *principle*. The only way for anti-Marketeers to argue with Callaghan was to try to show in detail that he was departing from the manifesto, and this moved the debate to precisely the ground where Callaghan felt strongest in Commons debates: his pragmatic, topic-by-topic approach to re-negotiation. These were battles which an experienced, well-briefed Parliamentarian like Callaghan could win, whatever the true merits of his case.

This explains why the most effective—or at least the most coherent—left-wing opposition to Callaghan came not from MPs but from the research staff at Transport House, Labour's headquarters. During the re-negotiations Transport House shadowed each Callaghan speech, statement and press conference, and prepared regular reports for a special Labour Party monitoring committee. These reports did what MPs found they could not do in full-dress debates: minutely dissect the details of Callaghan's progress.

In early July 1974, the Transport House staff wrote a paper drawing attention to the shift of emphasis between Callaghan's speeches in April and June: 'The office feels concern at some of the phrases used, and items of principle omitted, in the Government's June 4 statement. Although the Foreign Secretary has said that the April 1 statement stands as the principal statement of policy, none the less the office feels it is necessary to raise for discussion items for concern ... The June 4 statement does not mention the words "sovereignty" or "retention of powers by Parliament". In accepting the need for Community rules in industrial and regional policies the statement appears to accept a diminution of Parliament's powers in these fields.'

One thing Callaghan's 4 June speech *did* discuss was the Common Market budget. Transport House commented: 'The unfairness to Britain which is inherent in the EEC budget is twofold: under the present terms of membership, the United Kingdom faces the prospect of paying a disproportionately high share of the revenue *and* receiving an unduly low share of Community expenditure ... The Foreign Secretary laid most of the emphasis on the contribution side ... The impression was given that the negotiations on the specific subject of the budget would not go into detail on the pattern of Community expenditure.'

To Callaghan's great annoyance this report was leaked to *The Times*, which published it in full. He complained that it was 'intolerable' to re-negotiate with such backstairs sniping going on. But in the furore Callaghan did not reply to the specific points which Transport House had raised. He preferred to defend his actions on the rather less demanding occasions of a Commons debate or a press conference.

The actual process of re-negotiation was conducted between June 1974 and March 1975. Callaghan did most of it himself, although one of his Ministers of State, Roy Hattersley, negotiated the main deal on regional aid. The Cabinet gave Callaghan the nearest he could expect to a free hand: apart from two weekend meetings at Chequers, when he brought other ministers up-to-date with his progress, he was left to get the best terms he could, without interference. Once a fortnight, on average, he flew to Brussels (occasionally some other capital), and plunged into detailed arguments about the EEC budget, or the common agricultural policy, or special arrangements for Commonwealth countries. It was an arduous process, but one for which Callaghan, with his particular skills, was ideally suited. He could bluster, bargain, attack, retreat—and he knew exactly when and how to do each to the best effect. The other foreign ministers might get irritated by his constant reference back to 'what the British people will accept', but they recognised it as a consummate negotiating device in a consummate politician.

By October Callaghan was sufficiently confident that the re-negotiations would succeed to include in Labour's pledges for that month's General Election a promise to give the electorate an opportunity within twelve months to vote on British membership of the EEC. In the same month came the first hard evidence that the public would vote to stay in, *if* the Government recommended the re-negotiated terms to the people. Up to this point, opinion polls had shown a small but persistent majority of voters wanting to leave the Common Market. Pro-Market ministers rationalised this by saying, 'We have persuaded Callaghan; Callaghan will persuade Harold; Harold will persuade the Cabinet; and the Cabinet will persuade the people.' Now, Gallup Polls showed that they might be right. As usual, it found a four-to-three majority against the Market when it asked the standard question: 'If you could vote tomorrow on whether we should stay in the Common Market or leave it, how would you vote?' But then Gallup asked a second question: 'If the Government negotiated new terms for Britain's membership of the Common Market and they thought it was in Britain's interest to remain a member, how would you vote then—to stay in or to leave it?' This question produced a very different answer: a 2–1 majority for staying in.

At the same time, the polls showed there was little public knowledge of the way the EEC worked, or the details of re-negotiation. It appear that the mythical average voter's attitude went something like this: 'I do not think Britain was right to join the Common Market, and I have a feeling we would be better off outside. But if the Government feels really strongly that it would be dangerous to leave now, then I shall vote to stay in.' This kind of public feeling suited Callaghan well, for it meant that the currency of domestic debate would be security and reassurance, rather than the details of the re-negotiated terms—a quagmire to which Callaghan had deftly led Labour anti-Marketeers, and in which he subsequently left them.

Labour's retention of power in the October 1974 General Election—with a barely visible overall majority, but a comfortable 42-seat lead over the Conservatives—made Callaghan even more certain that he could keep both Britain in Europe and Labour in harness. On 15 October, five days after the General Election, he flew to Luxembourg and announced that he would like to see the re-negotiations completed by the following spring. The most difficult aspect of the re-negotiations—revision of the EEC's budget arrangements—was nearing solution. It would not be quite what Callaghan wanted ('what you pay is related to your capacity to pay—not a bad socialist principle'), but it would be near enough to enable him to satisfy the Cabinet.

The re-negotiations were completed ahead of schedule. The prime ministers and foreign ministers of the nine EEC countries met in Dublin over the weekend of 8–9 March, 1975, and Wilson and Callaghan returned to London to sell the new terms to the Cabinet, Parliament and the electorate. (Wilson's principal contribution in Dublin had been to extract a slightly better deal for New Zealand butter: one of the few consistent features of Wilson's career has been his concern for the Commonwealth.) The decisive Cabinet meeting was to be held ten days later, on 18 March, but in the meantime Callaghan left no doubts about his own attitude. Questioned in the Commons on 12 March, he said: 'A number of changes have been made during the course of the last twelve months in the policies of the EEC. As a result of our presence there and the activities of a number of British ministers, it has become more outward-looking than before and has embarked upon policies bound to be of help to the developing world.' Asked what would happen if the referendum verdict was for withdrawal, Callaghan replied: 'I would not wish to embark upon [that] thorny path . . . but clearly it would be a traumatic experience if we had to re-negotiate our way out, having re-negotiated our way in.'

Callaghan may have prejudged the Cabinet's decision, but he prejudged it accurately. On 18 March, the Cabinet approved the new terms by 16 votes to 7.

As in July 1974, the most telling criticisms of Callaghan's work came from the staff at Transport House. After the Dublin summit they prepared a 10,000 word 'Appraisal of the Terms', which sharply diverged from the Government's White Paper, 'Membership of the European Community; Report on Renegotiation', prepared around the same time. On point after point they disagreed on whether the Government had fulfilled Labour's manifesto promises of February 1974.

On reforming the *common agricultural policy*, the White Paper said: 'We are likely to remain net contributors to the cost of CAP, but we should now be able to contain the cost within reasonable limits.' Transport House said: 'Comparatively little progress has been made on this point.'

On *food prices*, the White Paper said: 'Prices in the United Kingdom have recently been no higher on balance than they would have been if we had remained outside the Community.' Transport House argued that 'import levies have been rising and British consumers are already paying more for their food as a result'.

On the final agreement reached in Dublin concerning the *EEC budget*, the White Paper said the UK would receive a refund 'if in any year our contribution goes significantly beyond what is fair in relation to our share of total Community gross national product'. Transport House said: 'The formula finally agreed in Dublin is on the whole decidedly less favourable to Britain than that proposed earlier by the [European] Commission.'

On *regional policy*, the White Paper said the EEC 'will allow the UK to pursue effective regional policies adjusted to the particular needs of individual areas of the country.' Transport House said: 'The powers of the Commission to interfere with [regional and industrial] grants remain unaltered.'

On control of *capital movements*, the White Paper said: 'In practice the Government can act to control capital movements when necessary.' Transport House recalled a specific manifesto objective ('We need an agreement on capital movements which protects our balance of payments and full employment policies') and observed: 'The subject of capital movements was not pursued by Mr Callaghan in his statement in the Council of Ministers last June, and does not appear to have featured in the re-negotiations since then.'

The Government and Transport House staff also disagreed on other points, like economic and monetary union, and on the value of the new terms to underdeveloped countries. In the end the Government conceded only one issue of substance where re-negotiation had failed—over national powers to control private steel investment. Transport House, on the other hand, was arguing that the re-negotiation was not fundamental (as had been promised), nor was it satisfactory, and on some points it was non-existent.

On 19 March, the day after the Cabinet had decided to recommend the new terms, the Transport House document came before the Labour Party's EEC Liaison Sub-Committee. Here the convention that ministers are rude about each other only in

Cabinet or at off-the-record briefings for journalists, comprehensively broke down. Callaghan did not arrive until halfway through the meeting, so the pro-Market case had to be led at first by his Minister of State Roy Hattersley, and the Agriculture Secretary Fred Peart. Lined up against them were three of the most strongly anti-Market ministers, Peter Shore, Tony Benn and Judith Hart. The other fourteen people present—back-bench MPs, trade unionists and Transport House staff—watched with bemused curiosity as the bitterness among the ministers exploded. An eavesdropper that evening at the door of Interview Room J, in the basement of the House of Commons, might well have concluded that the Labour Government was experiencing terminal convulsions.

The argument was waged paragraph by paragraph. Hattersley denounced the Transport House document for its inaccuracy. He said, for example, that articles 108 and 109 of the Treaty of Rome allowed Britain to restrict capital movements indefinitely, contrary to what the document said in one place; he wanted the statement changed. Shore replied that nothing needed changing: the statement was totally accurate, for Britain could not impose capital controls at will, without violating at least the spirit of the Treaty, which only allowed such controls at times of balance of payments difficulties.

When Callaghan did arrive at the meeting he admitted that he had not read the Transport House document—but then proceeded to join in the pro-Marketeers' denunciation of it. The most serious conflict concerned North Sea oil, for it raised an issue of fundamental importance for the British economy: would Britain retain control over pricing policy—for example by selling the oil in Britain at slightly below world prices if the Government thought this best for its energy and trade policies? When Ian Mikardo—the veteran left-wing MP with whom Callaghan had been allied in the mid-1940s—raised this point, Callaghan replied that the position was 'unclear'; Britain, he said was trying to secure a general worldwide pricing agreement through the International Energy Agency. Shore said this had nothing to do with the question Mikardo had asked; then Benn, supporting Shore, argued that Callaghan did not understand EEC rules. Far from being 'unclear', the situation was simple: no country could supply oil to one country, even itself, more cheaply than it supplied it to other EEC countries. When Benn finished making his point, Shore intervened once more: the Common Market's competition rules, he said, meant that Britain would be acting illegally if it altered the price of North Sea oil for the home market. Faced with this barrage from his Cabinet colleagues, Callaghan eventually retreated; what Shore had said, he conceded, was 'probably true'.

Later in the meeting, Callaghan and Benn clashed again, over sovereignty. The sub-committee minutes recorded the exchange: 'Mr Benn said that what had been omitted from the discussion was that the Commission's powers were enforceable in EEC and British courts against the British Government. For the first time, British courts could be enforcing an external law against the law of Parliament. We might reach the situation in which appeals were going to the House of Lords, which would allow the House of Lords permanently to frustrate the House of Commons. Mr Callaghan said that such an argument between Parliament and the courts was an extreme situation. He agreed that the powers did exist but in practice such a position would not be reached. When a state stood on its rights, the Commission backed away.'

By the end of the meeting Callaghan could contain his temper no longer. 'Some of you people are never satisfied,' he said, looking at the anti-Marketeers. 'I could have got everything the manifesto wanted, and more, and still you would snipe at what we've done.' And as the meeting dispersed, Callaghan was heard to mutter to himself: 'This document is a disgrace—a disgrace to research—a disgrace.' What had upset him more than anything else was that he had expected the meeting to be a general bun-fight over the well-worn arguments of EEC membership; he had come entirely unprepared to defend his re-negotiations in such detail. He had been caught out at the meeting, and he knew it.

Callaghan subsequently issued a rebuttal of the Transport House paper, arguing that it 'does not constitute a fair appraisal of what has been achieved in the re-negotiations. It is inaccurate or misleading on some major points.' Callaghan said that the common agricultural policy had been improved, that Transport House had got its sums wrong on the EEC budget, and that the interests of underdeveloped countries had been safeguarded by the Lomé Convention, which gave preferential trading terms to forty-six

Commonwealth and other third world countries. (Callaghan's argument on this point was challenged by the minister who had actually negotiated the Lomé Convention, Judith Hart. Admittedly a strong anti-Marketeer, she maintained that she could have done more for the third world had Britain stayed outside the EEC.)

But these were not now grounds Callaghan wanted to fight on. For him, membership of the EEC was important not so much for its detailed impact on the British economy or on the trading opportunities for underdeveloped countries, but for the part it played in the grander scheme of world affairs. Interviewed by *The Times* at the end of March 1975, he said of Britain's role in the world: 'It is based on the influence we exert mainly through our membership of international organisations such as the United Nations, the Commonwealth, the European Community, the International Monetary Fund . . . Of all the ministerial posts I have held, [being Foreign Secretary] is the one I find literally enjoyable.'

Callaghan was now saying something close to what the pro-Marketeers had preached all along: their case for British membership of the EEC had little to do with the price of butter or the power to control capital movements; they were more concerned with the idea of European harmony and the tide of world history. But what Callaghan understood better then most is that voters care more for material success; whereas Heath had almost boasted about the material price Britain would have to pay for achieving harmony, Callaghan's great achievement was to persuade the public that harmony—with its attendant blessings of peace, security, and a brave new world for our grandchildren—was practically free. And with the referendum date fixed for 5 June, Callaghan approached the campaign with the special enthusiasm of the convert.

Callaghan's first task was to minimise the potential damage to Labour that could be caused by anti-Market feeling inside the party. His brushes with Transport House had warned him that an organised national campaign by the Labour Party outside Parliament could make life highly uncomfortable for him. There was little he could do to prevent the party expressing its majority anti-Market view at a special conference scheduled for 26 April: his task was to prevent the party from doing anything too active afterwards, in the referendum campaign itself.

The route to neutralising the special conference passed through the NEC, which met on 26 March to draw up a resolution for the conference. Beforehand, Wilson and Callaghan let it be known—by those strange smoke signals which count technically as private hints, but which ensure massive media coverage—that they would resign if the party campaigned openly against the Government. The move worked; for when the NEC—inevitably—voted to recommend British withdrawal from the Common Market, the party's general secretary Ron Hayward added two crucial riders. First, the party was short of cash, so there would be little money for a national campaign; secondly, 'the right to differ' should apply to party members who opposed the NEC's anti-Market line, just as it applied to Government ministers who opposed the Cabinet's pro-Market line. Hayward's statement had exactly the effect Callaghan and Wilson wanted: the party's voice would be muted.

The special conference on 26 April became little more than a ritual. Callaghan was careful to distinguish his view from the out-and-out pro-Marketeers, but he could still not completely hide his enthusiasm: 'The question is not whether the Community is an ideal institution. We have to take it or leave it knowing that even if it is unsatisfactory in some ways, it nevertheless has the capacity for change and flexibility. The question to be decided is whether on balance Britain's interest is better served if we remain a member than if we leave. After twelve months' experience I have reached the conclusion that it is better for us to stay: better for the British people, better for the people of the Commonwealth, better for the future of Europe.'

Callaghan's speech may have swayed a few delegates from the constituencies, but the overall result had been determined in advance of the conference by the block votes of the trade unions. The conference voted by 3,724,000 votes to 1,986,000 in favour of withdrawal from the EEC, but Hayward's statement on party activity remained. The Labour lion had roared; its teeth, however, had all been drawn.

Callaghan took little part in the referendum campaign itself; on the few occasions when he did speak, he followed the same line as his speech to the special conference—that after a long period weighing up the issues, he now considered British membership a Good Thing.

Privately, he was more active. Most mornings at 9.30 he would chair a ministerial 'Referendum Steering Group' meeting at the Foreign Office. The group consisted of the main pro-Market ministers, like Shirley Williams, David Ennals and Roy Hattersley: the prominent exception was Roy Jenkins who was considered too committed to the non-Government 'Britain in Europe' campaign to play a proper role in the government group. Participants in the group recall how Callaghan briskly conducted its business, ensuring that the agenda was completed by 10.30, when there would often be Cabinet meetings at 10 Downing Street.

The steering group had little of the anxiety which attends Labour (or Conservative) campaign meetings during general elections. Both the published polls, and the private polls which the group commissioned from Market & Opinion Research International (MORI), confirmed that there would be a two-to-one 'Yes' majority—a figure which barely changed throughout the campaign. But beyond this basic fact, the polls showed how precisely Callaghan had judged the mood of voters. While they were often baffled by details, the general attitudes discovered by the polls were those which Callaghan had been articulating: MORI found that a majority of voters thought that Britain's voice in Europe had been much stronger since re-negotiation; that the Government had done a good job in its re-negotiations; that the Commonwealth wanted Britain to stay in the EEC; and that it was important to 'our children's future' to stay in.

The polls also confirmed that Callaghan's *style* was right. On 16 May, Robert Worcester, MORI's managing director, wrote to the steering group: 'When you are ahead (as we are) you reassure people and encourage them to cast their vote. It is not the time to frighten them with the spectre of communism, fear of the consequences of a No vote, or bogeymen.' Callaghan was too experienced a politician to indulge in counter-productive scare tactics; on the contrary, reassurance was his most evident stock-in-trade.

The voting on 5 June went as predicted, with a 67 per cent 'Yes' vote. Callaghan had achieved both his objectives: he kept Britain in the Common Market, and he prevented the Labour Party from splitting down the middle. He had set out to silence the anti-Marketeers by agreeing to their call for a referendum; by winning the referendum vote so conclusively he had done just that.

*

On one occasion after the referendum, Callaghan's skills in handling the Common Market deserted him. An international energy conference was planned to take place in December 1975; but in an attempt to keep the conference down to manageable size, arrangements were made for twenty-seven participants. The EEC would have one seat. In October, the Common Market foreign ministers met in Brussels to decide a joint policy. At one point during the meeting, when everything seemed to be going smoothly, one of Callaghan's senior Foreign Office officials, Michael Butler, slipped out of the room for a break. A few moments later a more junior official rushed out to call Butler back; 'the Foreign Secretary has gone mad', he said.

When Butler returned to the meeting he found it in a state of some disorder. For, without telling anyone beforehand—not even his own officials—Callaghan had demanded that Britain should have a separate seat of her own at the energy conference. Callaghan's argument had some force: Britain was the one major energy *producer* in the EEC, and soon to become an oil exporter—so Britain's interests were different from those of the other EEC countries which were primarily energy *consumers*. On the other hand, the twenty-seven seats which had been allocated for the conference had been distributed with great diplomatic care. It would be impossible simply to make Britain the twenty-eighth participant, for the oil-producing states, and the third-world countries, and sub-groups among them would all insist on increasing their quota of seats also.

For six weeks Callaghan maintained his demand, to the irritation both of his British Cabinet colleagues and of his EEC partners. 'How are you going to get Jim off the hook?' one journalist asked Harold Wilson during a private briefing. 'I don't know,' came the reply; 'He got himself on it. He can get himself off it.'

Eventually Callaghan compromised by taking part in the conference as a member of the EEC team—but with the opportunity to talk separately for two minutes about Britain's special interests. In the event he spoke for twelve minutes, causing Wilson to remark afterwards: 'Mr Callaghan may not have hit the moon, but he has had a good crack at reaching Snowdon's peak.'

15

1976
The Fight for
Wilson's Crown

'The question is,' said Alice, 'whether you can make words mean so many different things.'
'The question is,' said Humpty Dumpty, 'which is to be master—that is all.'

—LEWIS CARROLL, *Through the Looking Glass*

The most surprising thing about Harold Wilson's resignation as Prime Minister is that it should have been a surprise at all. During the October 1974 general election campaign he had talked privately, but widely, about retiring after two years of his second term at Number Ten; since he had become Prime Minister again in March 1974, this suggested that hopeful successors should tune up their political muscles for a leadership contest in the spring of 1976.

By the end of 1975 the message was becoming stronger. Wilson made up his mind to retire on or near his sixtieth birthday—11 March, 1976—and shortly before Christmas he formally notified his intention to the Queen and the Speaker of the House of Commons, George Thomas. Thomas has always been a close friend of Callaghan—both men have been Cardiff MPs since 1945—and there has been some suggestion that Wilson, in telling Thomas, was obliquely letting Callaghan know his intentions. There is, however, no evidence that Thomas broke the confidence: on the contrary, Wilson himself told Callaghan in December 1975 that he was 'considering' resigning.

The problem was that Callaghan did not believe him. 'The Prime Minister has been saying he will retire shortly', he remarked to one astonished British ambassador abroad in the New Year.

'He told me again last week. But you know, I look at the calendar and I see the Queen's Jubilee coming [in 1977], and the Commonwealth Prime Ministers' Conference, and the first European summit in London. And I say to myself, surely the little beggar won't pass up those.'

In its modest way, it was like Callaghan's failure to anticipate Turkey's invasion of Cyprus—or Israel's failure to anticipate Egypt's attack across the Suez Canal in October 1973: the facts were known, but rejected for being inconsistent with previously held ideas. So when Wilson opened the Cabinet meeting on 16 March with the words, 'Before we come to Parliamentary business I want to make a brief statement...', Callaghan was only half prepared: Wilson had told him only a few minutes earlier that the resignation announcement was imminent.

The leadership battle that followed was without constitutional precedent. Technically, members of the Parliamentary Labour Party were choosing a new party leader. In fact, of course, they were electing a new Prime Minister as well. All previous Labour and Conservative leadership ballots had taken place in opposition; now a ballot was being conducted by a party in power.

This gave Callaghan an immediate advantage. Internal party battles in opposition are usually about policies and sometimes about principles. In government, these considerations tend to be subordinated to the more practical matter of staying in power. Callaghan could not market a strong line in policies or principles: he offered himself specifically as the man who could hold the party together and give it the best chance of winning the next General Election.

Such a marketing pitch, however, poses certain problems. One involves the theology of power-versus-principle; but Callaghan did not worry about this, partly because he never does, and partly because few MPs who maintained that only a left-wing Labour Government could be a successful Labour Government would ever vote for Callaghan anyway. The more serious problem was this: how do you campaign against other candidates, some of whom have clear political philosophies, when you have none—and furthermore, how do you avoid being drawn into divisive arguments when the essence of your appeal is unity?

Callaghan's answer was dazzlingly simple: he said nothing. He issued no statements about the contest, made no speeches about it, and gave no interviews. He paraded himself not as a candidate, but as Her Majesty's Principal Secretary of State for Foreign and Commonwealth Affairs. At the height of the first ballot, on 22 March, he dominated media coverage first by welcoming Andrei Gromyko, the Soviet Foreign Minister, to London, and then appearing in the House of Commons to warn Rhodesia that 'Mr Smith is leading his country on the path of death and destruction. Even at this late stage I ask the European population of Rhodesia to believe that there is an alternative path . . . that the time is here when the legitimate aspirations of the African people can be met . . .' As Ian Aitken reported in the next day's *Guardian*: 'Mr Callaghan yesterday played what his supporters regard as his strongest card in the battle for the Premiership—the ostentatious posture of the elder statesman of the Labour Party, and therefore the natural successor to Mr Wilson.'

Meanwhile, Callaghan's lieutenants lobbied Labour MPs for support. The lieutenants themselves reflected the coalition of party factions which Callaghan had marshalled during his career: John Golding and Tom Urwin were strong members of the trade union group of Labour MPs; John Cunningham was the son of Andrew Cunningham who had at one time been an important ally of Callaghan on the Labour Party NEC. Ted Rowlands was the MP for Merthyr Tydfil, in the heart of Callaghan's Welsh power-base; Edmund Marshall was a left-wing MP who thought Callaghan would stand up to the right; James Wellbeloved was a right-wing MP who thought Callaghan would stand up to the left. And the organiser of the group was Merlyn Rees, an MP with a strong personal loyalty towards Callaghan, deriving from Rees's term as Under-Secretary to Callaghan at the Home Office from 1968 to 1970.

The significant point about this group is that it was so heterogeneous. The members did not represent a theory of what the Labour Party was about, or where it should be heading; instead they represented a series of credits that Callaghan had built up—in Wales, with the unions, in the party, and among individuals. The time had now come to cash these credits in.

*

Callaghan's five opponents acted differently. Each of them defended and explained their candidacy in public and one, Tony Benn, issued daily policy statements on subjects ranging from economic strategy to open government. Roy Jenkins and Anthony Crosland went almost as far by articulating their—well-known—political philosophies; Denis Healey stood as the iron Chancellor who knew how to deal with the unions; and Michael Foot walked his dog on Hampstead Heath, not so much baring his left-wing soul as reminding people that it was still there, somewhere.

Labour MPs, then, had a wide choice of candidates and campaigning styles; the one thing they had in common was that all except Foot had more Cabinet experience than any previous Labour leader at the time of his election.

The leadership contest was not just about the nature of the candidates, however; it was also about the nature of the Parliamentary Labour Party. MPs lined up along various axes: right–left; pro-Market–anti-Market; young–old; worker–intellectual. Some of these reflected old divisions, notably age and ideology. But the Common Market controversy was more recent; and the proportions of workers and intellectuals had changed sharply since Callaghan first entered Parliament in 1945. Then for every ten Labour MPs with university degrees, twelve counted themselves as rank-and-file workers. By 1976, there were only five rank-and-file workers for every ten university-educated MPs.

The variety of cross-currents within the PLP is important, as the voting system for party leader means that the eventual winner must secure the support of a majority of MPs—unlike, say, when a candidate stands for election as an MP in a local constituency, where the first-past-the-post system means that MPs are frequently elected on minority votes. And in the 1976 Labour leadership contest, the voting system critically affected the outcome; it ultimately helped the man who had made the fewest enemies, at the expense of the man who made the most friends.

The result of the first ballot was announced to Labour MPs at 6 p.m. on 25 March. Foot led with 90 votes, followed by Callaghan 84, Jenkins 56, Benn 37, Healey 30, and Crosland 17. In a first-past-the-post ballot this would have given Foot victory, even though he had won the votes of less than one in three Labour MPs. Under

Labour's rules of voting by exhaustive ballot, however, more rounds would be needed.

Crosland, with the lowest vote, was eliminated, and Benn immediately announced that he would withdraw voluntarily in favour of Foot.

For twenty minutes Callaghan sat in his room at the House of Commons with his lieutenants and contemplated the prospect of defeat. The arithmetic of their gloom went like this: Foot would inevitably secure enough votes in round two to be left in the play-off. Callaghan was confident he could defeat Foot—but he had to get through to the final round himself to have the chance. Suppose Crosland's 17 votes went to Jenkins—and suppose Healey, like Benn, withdrew, and his 30 votes also went to Jenkins. In that case, Callaghan would be squeezed out of the play-off, which would become a straight right–left, Jenkins–Foot battle. 'It gradually dawned on us', recalled one MP at the meeting, 'that we could lose after all.'

The gloom was lifted by a knock at the door. It was Dr Dickson Mabon, one of Jenkins's campaign managers; he had come to report that Jenkins was withdrawing from the race. 'From that moment on', says one Callaghan man, 'I think Jim started forming his Cabinet. He knew he didn't have to worry any more.'

Jenkins's surprise decision was due to the simple fact that he had won 12 votes fewer than even his most pessimistic prediction. But this in turn reflected a more fundamental failure in Jenkins's campaign. Of all senior Labour politicians, he was the most fervently pro-Market; while this ensured majority support—though only just—among the 90 strongly pro-Market Labour MPs, it also denied him all but a handful of neutral and anti-Market votes. Evidence collected by the *Sunday Times* and the London Weekend Television programme *Weekend World* from more than 250 MPs during the contest, suggests that Jenkins won only seven votes from the 227 Labour MPs who were *not* passionate pro-Marketeers. Contrary to the fears of the Callaghan camp, for Jenkins to have stayed in the race would have been an act of insane hope rather than calculated judgement: his enemies in the centre and on the left of the party massively outweighed his friends on the right.

Healey, on the other hand, refused to withdraw; so three

candidates went forward to the second round. Callaghan now began to reap the advantages of his standing in the party as the man with the fewest enemies. While Foot collected almost all of Benn's vote, together with a handful of Jenkins's supporters who preferred Foot's libertarianism, Callaghan took most of Jenkins's and Crosland's votes. Callaghan had become the reluctant choice of the centre and right as the only man who could stop Foot. When the result of the second ballot was announced on 30 March, Callaghan had taken the lead, with 141 votes to Foot's 133 and Healey's 38.

The final ballot was almost a formality. One or two Foot supporters vainly hoped that Healey might give his public support to their man; their reasoning for this improbable event was that Foot and Healey were the two men who had worked together to secure the £6 pay limit agreement with the TUC the previous summer. Healey, to nobody else's surprise, kept his own counsel, and most of his votes duly transferred to Callaghan. The result of the third ballot was announced by George Strauss, the 'Father' of the House of Commons and chief scrutineer of the PLP: at 4 p.m. on 5 April, in the Grand Committee Room, he told Labour MPs that James Callaghan was elected their new leader. He had defeated Foot by 176 votes to 137.

Callaghan rose to speak. After the roar of cheers subsided, he said: '. . . I want no cliques. There will be no insiders or outsiders. So far as the past is concerned, I shall wipe the slate clean and I ask everyone else to do the same, and that includes the members of the self-appointed groups in the House. I mean especially the Tribune group and the Manifesto group. None of you holds the Ark of the Covenant. The party workers in the country expect your first loyalty to be not to your group meetings but to the party meetings. I shall not be willing to accept a situation in which minority groups in the Parliamentary Labour Party manœuvre in order to foist their views on the party as a whole.'

Thus Callaghan began his term as Labour leader, not with a warm appeal for party unity but with a stern warning against party disunity. In speaking this way, Callaghan tacitly acknowledged the curious amalgam of MPs who had chosen him as their leader. If a nominee of the right or left had won, the victor would probably have reaffirmed his beliefs while diplomatically offering reconciliation to the opposing faction. If some overwhelmingly popular man had commanded the enthusiastic support from all sections of the party, he would have needed to say very little. But Callaghan was not overwhelmingly popular—most of the votes which finally gave him victory were second or third round votes—and he knew that he was not altogether trusted by either the right or left of the party. He had done well among Scottish and Welsh MPs, among MPs who were sponsored by the General and Municipal Workers' Union and the National Union of Mineworkers; he had held his own among younger MPs and those with degrees; he had done badly among MPs with marginal constituencies. But above all, he became leader for a singularly negative reason—that a large number of MPs considered him the less undesirable candidate when the only alternative was Michael Foot. For a man whose political career had been largely anchored to the ideals of party unity and support for the leader of the day, it was an uncertain basis on which to construct a new unity now he was himself leader.

Callaghan made his speech to MPs as leader of the Labour Party—Harold Wilson was still, formally, Prime Minister. But shortly afterwards, Wilson drove to Buckingham Palace to resign. Soon after 6 p.m. James Callaghan became Britain's new Prime Minister.

Just as Callaghan started out as Labour leader by warning MPs against disunity, he started out as Prime Minister by warning the public about the economy. In a television broadcast on the evening of his appointment, he said: 'I emphasise to you that if we fail to bring down inflation, we shall never succeed in overcoming unemployment. We cannot have a prosperous industry in this country if we are unable to sell our goods overseas . . . We are still not earning the standard of living we are enjoying. We are only keeping up our standards by borrowing, and this cannot go on indefinitely.' Callaghan's tone then changed abruptly: 'Well, that sounds a gloomy start. But it is not all gloomy. Britain is a country that can have a great future.' The remainder of his speech comprised homely, undemanding and uncontroversial truths about the need to fight for Good against Evil ('Let us root out injustice ... let us have honesty and fair dealing ... Let us be enemies of vandalism and violence.'). Two brief passages, however, gave a clue to his inner emotions. The first was an appeal to young people: 'Play a full part in our efforts. It will be your world. Help us to build it.' The second was an appeal to older viewers: 'You and I have lived through good and bad days in our country's history, but this country has survived such periods before and emerged greater in the end. So let those of us who are older encourage and help those who are younger, urge them to rebuild Britain again upon secure foundations.'

Callaghan had begun to draft this speech while the leadership contest was still in progress. Discussing with a close friend what he should write, Callaghan spoke of his eight grandchildren, whom he adores, and said: 'It is their world I am working for. My job will be to lead the people out of Egypt and into the desert. I doubt if I shall live to see the Promised Land.'

Callaghan's sentiments may have been a little mawkish, but they were genuine; more to the point, they were realistic. There could be no greater contrast with the early boast of his predecessor, Wilson, in 1963 that 'we are re-defining and we are re-stating our Socialism in terms of the scientific revolution'. Whatever mistakes Callaghan was going to make as Prime Minister, that was one kind of hostage on which his fortunes would emphatically not depend.

16

The Prime Minister We Deserve?

'I want our administration, not only to make Britain economically healthier, but to make it a society with greater fairness and greater social justice.'
—JAMES CALLAGHAN, in a televised address to the nation, 5 April 1976

The Peter Principle states that men and women are promoted progressively through jobs they can perform, until they reach a job which is beyond their capacity—their 'level of incompetence'. There they stick.

James Callaghan apparently reached his level of incompetence in 1964, when he became Chancellor of the Exchequer. His election as Labour Party leader and Prime Minister in 1976 suggests that the principle should be regarded with some scepticism, at least when applied to politics. But Callaghan's eventual success in reaching Number Ten also requires a more specific explanation.

Certainly, Callaghan's record in office contains more failures than triumphs. While all judgements are subjective, we suspect that many people would broadly agree with the following checklist. Failures: economic and monetary policy 1964–7; immigration policy 1968; the handling of the Parliamentary Boundaries dispute 1969; the Cyprus crisis 1974; the 'cod war' with Iceland 1975–6. Successes: tax reform and international monetary reform 1964–7; policy towards demonstrations 1968–70; policy towards southern Africa 1974–6. On Ulster (1967–70) it is fair to say that he has been the least unsuccessful minister in recent years to handle the issue. And whether you regard the Common Market re-negotiations as a brilliant tactical achievement, or an unparalleled disaster, depends largely on your attitudes towards the Common Market itself.

Callaghan's rivals for the Labour leadership could each claim a more successful, or at any rate less flawed, ministerial record. But in two respects Callaghan, the tortoise, outdistanced all the hares. In the first place he was much better known and liked among Labour voters—possibly because he had simply been around and in the public eye more than the other candidates, without alienating too many of them. (Labour *activists* were more inclined to support Foot or Benn.) Following a MORI opinion poll during the leadership contest which discovered this fact, Bob Worcester commented in the *Sunday Times*: 'Callaghan is the man acceptable to all sides. With the cracks in the party so evident, he seems to be the one paper-hanger who can paste it together.'

Callaghan's second asset, however, was probably more crucial. More than any other candidate, he had cultivated friends, allies and supporters *where they were needed*—among MPs, within Transport House, and among the unions which consistently voted him as party Treasurer. The previous chapter recounted how the breadth of Callaghan's support specifically helped him win the leadership contest. And while there may be some justice in the complaint of Callaghan's opponents that his support was like an estuary—'wide but shallow'—he could nevertheless mobilise enough of it when it mattered.

The cause of this phenomenon is also the cause of the most serious doubts about Callaghan's ability to succeed as Prime Minister. For against his poor record in government must be set his outstanding record in opposition—during the periods of formal opposition from 1951 to 1964, and from 1970 to 1974; but also during the battle over *In Place of Strife*, when Callaghan became in effect a one-man opposition inside the Cabinet. Callaghan's skills are supremely the skills of opposition—and the support from which he draws his power derives overwhelmingly from a recognition of those skills. Above all, Callaghan has applied rigorously Harold Laski's injunctions to secure consent, and to perform the role of broker of ideas. Callaghan found in opposition that while many other people were thinking new thoughts, he could usefully put out an anchor to windward and ensure that the boat of Labour policy-making did not get blown too far from the shores of party unity and electoral consent.

A less kind way of putting this is to say that Callaghan's peculiar talent is to discover the lowest common denominator, and that for him this is more a state of mind than just a tactic. Yet such a talent can be invaluable, especially for a Labour politician in opposition when other people are incapable of finding any common denominator at all. It is, however, a talent which is insufficient for government, let alone for a Prime Minister; success in office requires more positive virtues than does success in opposition.

Callaghan's supporters paint a distinctly more optimistic picture of his chances of doing well as Prime Minister. 'In a fashion that is true of no other candidate,' said one ministerial enthusiast during the 1976 leadership campaign, 'Jim cares about the Labour movement: those dreary committee rooms, the bad teas, the duplicating machines that get ink everywhere, the old ladies writing notices with exasperating slowness. Jim *likes* all that.' According to this minister, Callaghan's closeness to his political roots gives him an instinct for doing the right things, when the more intellectually grounded attitudes of the other candidates might lead any of them towards disastrous decisions.

The obvious question is whether Callaghan's ministerial record can conceivably sustain this argument. One of Callaghan's colleagues in Downing Street maintains that his record should, to some extent, be discounted: 'How can you say of a man of sixty-four that he has matured in the last three or four years? But that is what has happened with Jim.' Even if these two observers are right, they at most construct a line of defence against attempts to judge Callaghan's future by analysing his past.

One close family friend offered the most extravagant—and Caesarian—forecast, by some margin, of Callaghan's Prime Ministerial performance. 'Sure, it is difficult to detect what Jim stands for by looking at his record. But consider Roosevelt and Churchill. Nobody knew what *they* really stood for until they reached the top of the greasy pole; both of them had chequered pasts, as Jim has. But people sensed that they had the qualities that were needed to lead their countries at a time of crisis. I believe Jim has the same qualities: he is tough, shrewd, and knows how to persuade people that firm policies are needed to ensure recovery. He is the sort of man to weather Britain's economic crisis, and keep the helm steady.'

Quite apart from the questionable comparison of Callaghan's personal qualities with those of Roosevelt and Churchill, one serious weakness in this argument is that it assumes that there is general agreement about the nature of Britain's crisis and how to get out of it—and that what you need is a man who can translate this agreed unity into action. A war leader can assume that the people share his determination to defeat a precisely identified enemy. But Britain's current problems are not like this. Except in the *simpliste* sense that everyone dislikes inflation, unemployment and low economic growth, there is widespread dispute over the real nature of Britain's problems, and the measures needed to overcome them.

In this situation, the ability to achieve consent is a necessary but far from sufficient talent in a Prime Minister. Indeed, as we observed in Chapter Three, the pursuit of party unity for its own sake is likely to result in random policies which have, at best, an evens chance of working. Creating consent is a good way of making a policy work: but relying on an existing consensus to decide what policy to follow in the first place can be dangerous.

There is, perhaps, one hope. We posed at the very beginning of this book the question, is Callaghan a Caesar or an anti-Caesar—a question which, now he is Prime Minister, can be roughly translated into: is he going to dictate policy from Number Ten, or continue in the role for which he is best suited—as a broker of ideas and of consent? If the cabinet ministers in his Government can jointly agree on policies that will work, then it is possible that Callaghan, as anti-Caesar, could be the man to win party, union and public acceptance for them.

Our own view is not hopeful. As we write, the responses of the Government to Britain's economic problems, and the pressures from abroad on sterling, are uncomfortably reminiscent of the spineless strategy of the last Labour Government ten years ago, when Callaghan was Chancellor of the Exchequer. Then the main economic debates concerned growth, the balance of payments and the role of sterling. The one coherent attempt to achieve growth— the National Plan—was sacrificed in a makeshift series of hire-purchase controls, credit restrictions and public expenditure cuts in a vain attempt to save the pound. Today, when the chief problems are inflation, unemployment and the reconstruction of Britain's manufacturing base, the Government has succeeded in reducing the rate of inflation from an annual rate of more than 30 per cent to 10–15 per cent; but otherwise the sterling crises, international loans and pressures to reduce public expenditure have an ominously familiar ring. And just as devaluation was not merely rejected for three years in the mid 1960s, but not even seriously discussed, so the Wilson–Callaghan Government since 1974 has not engaged in the basic arguments on (say) import controls. It remains likely that import controls will be introduced —but that, like devaluation, they will be prompted by the circumstances of crisis, rather than by the conviction of a carefully considered policy. This impression is reinforced by the attitude of left-wing ministers in July 1976 when the Cabinet decided to cut public expenditure by a further £1,000 million. Their acceptance of the cuts derived partly from a belief that these would not succeed for long in sustaining their chief objective—maintaining overseas confidence in sterling—and that the next crisis would make more radical policies inevitable.

More fundamentally, the levels of unemployment Britain has experienced since early 1975, and the acquiescence of the Wilson–Callaghan Government in most of the Treasury's demands, must raise serious doubts about the capacity of a Labour Government to achieve the changes in British society that it exists to secure.

It is, of course, possible to have more than one view about what the underlying purposes of a Labour Government are—and the variety of candidates for the party leadership in 1976 reflected something of the range of views. The criticism of Callaghan is not that he has the wrong vision, but that he has no vision at all. And during his first few weeks at Number Ten, he has shown few signs of encouraging, or even allowing, some coherent strategy to evolve from his cabinet colleagues, which he could then employ his considerable political skills to make work. Callaghan is faced with one traditional dilemma which confronts Labour administrations: should a crisis be an occasion for pushing forward with radical measures—or an excuse for postponing them? On his past record, Callaghan is a postponer rather than a pusher. And his actions in May 1976, when he and Healey robustly persuaded the Cabinet to shelve its plans for a new child benefits scheme—a major piece of social reform promised in two Labour election manifestos —suggest that Callaghan's style did not greatly change with his move to Number Ten.

*

Similar criticisms could be levelled against Harold Wilson as Prime Minister. Some leading Labour politicians even find Callaghan's style of leadership a refreshing improvement. Where Wilson was considered shifty ('There are two things I dislike about Harold', said one enemy: 'his face.'), Callaghan is seen by his ministerial colleagues as straightforward. One improbable source of praise is Tony Benn, who told friends during the early weeks of Callaghan's tenure, 'It's so unlike the old days, when Harold didn't hear what you wanted to say, but only calculated the tactics of the issue: Jim actually *listens.*'

Equally, Callaghan has carefully rebuilt bridges between the Government and Transport House. Where Wilson discouraged ministers from participating in 1975 and 1976 in study groups set up by the party's National Executive Committee, Callaghan decided at the end of May to reverse this attitude; he wrote to ministers specifically asking them to co-operate in party policy-making. On 28 July 1976, when Callaghan launched a new Social Contract, he did so having secured the ready co-operation of both the TUC and—more surprisingly—the Labour Party NEC.

But what conclusion should be drawn from Callaghan's new relationships with Benn, and with Transport House? The optimistic interpretation is that Callaghan, a man well aware of his own limitations, is genuinely seeking guidance for a strategy which will extract Labour from the depressing politics of aimless tactical manoeuvring. The pessimistic interpretation is that the trimmer is back at work, squaring the chaps, for the perfectly respectable reason of keeping the party together, but for no reason beyond that.

One day the optimistic interpretation may prove correct. Until then, we remain sceptical.

Selective Bibliography

In preparing this study we have consulted a wide variety of books and published and unpublished documents. No student of post-war Labour politics can get very far without access to such standard works as *Hansard*; the Labour Party annual conference *Reports*; *The Times Guide to the House of Commons*, published after each General Election; *The British General Election of . . .* series which since 1951 has been written under the direction of David Butler. Further books which assisted our research include:

BACON, Robert, and ELTIS, Walter. *Britain's Economic Problem: Too Few Producers*. Macmillan, 1976

BECKERMAN, Wilfred (ed.). *The Labour Government's Economic Record, 1964–1970*. Duckworth, 1972

BRANDON, Henry. *In the Red: The Struggle for Sterling, 1964–66*. André Deutsch, 1966

BRITTAN, Samuel. *Steering the Economy: The Role of the Treasury*. Secker & Warburg, 1969; Penguin, 1971

GEORGE-BROWN, Lord. *In My Way*. Gollancz, 1971; Penguin, 1972

BUTLER, David, and SLOMAN, Anne. *British Political Facts, 1900–1975*. Macmillan, 1975

BUTLER, David, and KITZINGER, Uwe. *The 1975 Referendum*. Macmillan, 1976

CALLAGHAN, James. *A House Divided: Northern Ireland Dilemma*. Collins, 1973

CROSSMAN, Richard. *The Diaries of a Cabinet Minister*, Vol. I. Hamish Hamilton and Cape, 1975

DALTON, Hugh. *High Tide and After: Memoirs, 1945–1960*. Muller, 1962

DONOGHUE, Bernard, and JONES, G. W. *Herbert Morrison: Portrait of a Politician*. Weidenfeld & Nicolson, 1973

FOOT, Michael. *Aneurin Bevan, 1945–1960*. Davis-Poynter, 1973

FOOT, Paul. *The Politics of Harold Wilson*. Penguin, 1968

HOWARD, Anthony, and WEST, Richard. *The Making of the Prime Minister*. Cape, 1965

HUMPHRY, Derek, and WARD, Michael. *Passports and Politics*. Penguin, 1974

HUNTER, Leslie. *The Road to Brighton Pier*. Arthur Barker, 1959

JENKINS, Peter. *The Battle of Downing Street*. Charles Knight, 1970

LAPPING, Brian. *The Labour Government, 1964–70*. Penguin, 1970

LASKI, Harold. *A Grammar of Politics*. Current edition Allen & Unwin, 1967

MCKENZIE, Robert. *British Political Parties*. Heinemann, 1953; Mercury Books, 1953

NORTON, Philip. *Dissension in the House of Commons, 1945–74*. Macmillan, 1975

POLYVIOU, Polyvios. *Cyprus in Search of a Constitution*. Nicosia

Sunday Times Insight Team. *Ulster*. Penguin, 1972

WIGG, Lord. *George Wigg*. Michael Joseph, 1972

WILLIAMS, Marcia. *Inside Number 10*. Weidenfeld & Nicolson, 1952

WILSON, Harold. *The Labour Government, 1964–1970: A Personal Record*. Weidenfeld & Nicolson, 1971; Penguin, 1974

Index